A BEGINNER'S LIFE

A BEGINNER'S LIFE

The Adventures of
Tom Phillips

Full Court Press
Englewood Cliffs, New Jersey

First Edition

Copyright © 2015 by Tom Phillips

Published in the United States of America
by Full Court Press, 601 Palisade Avenue
Englewood Cliffs, NJ 07632
fullcourtpressnj.com

ISBN 978-1-938812-53-8
Library of Congress Control No. 2015936062

Editing and Book Design by Barry Sheinkopf
for Bookshapers (bookshapers.com)
Cover art by Django Phillips
Colophon by Liz Sedlack

FOR MY CHILDREN, AND THEIR CHILDREN

ACKNOWLEDGEMENTS

Thanks to my daughter Cassia, who urged me to write down the stories I told about my childhood; to my sister-in-law Linda, who kept at me to continue; and to my wife Debra, who dug out the manuscript years later and pushed me to finish.

Thanks also to Deborah Burke and Ellen Ciporen, two early readers who contributed invaluable suggestions and criticism. Thanks to my son Django for the cover art, and Barry Sheinkopf for his expert editing.

Finally thanks to my late parents, William and Josephine, who raised me to write.

"Endlessly rise the distant mountains,
blue heaped upon blue."

—*Zen phrase*

TABLE OF CONTENTS

PART ONE

1:War Baby, *1*

2: Being An American, *13*

3: Confessions Of A Philo-Semite, *23*

4: Harvard Of The Midwest, *37*

5: Bound For Glory, *47*

6: Down And Out In San Francisco, *55*

7: Tom Phillips Reporting, *71*

8:On My Own, *86*

9: The Hot Seat, *95*

PART TWO

10: The Flaw In Zen, *109*

11: Mother Ganga, *121*

12: The Stumbling Block, *135*

13: The Groves Of Academe, *144*

14: 1989, *150*

15: Fish Family In A Big House, *162*

16: The African Explorer, *170*

17: A Little Lear, *180*

18: The Cup Of Trembling, *187*

19: The Road To Dotage, *198*

20: El Mundo, Señor, *206*

Epilogue: Apology, *210*

1

WAR BABY

My memory was born when I was two or three years old, in Montclair, New Jersey. We lived on the second floor, on a tree-lined street with a leafy view out the window. One morning I woke up early, to a light I'd never seen. It was a soft, luminous haze that seemed to roll in through the windows. Outside, a white haze was dancing on the surface of the leaves. The light seemed to come from just beyond the trees, or to rise from the air itself. The only sound was the birds.

The side of the crib was down, so I climbed out, wondering. Then I went across the hall to tell my mother. I walked around my father's side of the bed, stood next to her, and touched her arm, once, then twice.

Her eyes opened.

— Look, I said.

She pushed herself up, and stared wildly at me.

— What are you doing in here?

She stood up, huge and angry, pointing to the door, ordering me back to bed. She didn't look out the window.

I crept back across the hall and into the crib. The luminous haze brightened, resolved into day.

My only feeling was shock. I thought my mother, who loved me, would see things as I did, feel whatever I felt.

I was too little for ideas or conclusions. But the experience left me with two deep impressions: The world is full of unexpected beauty and mystery, and I was on my own in it.

I WAS BORN IN JANUARY 1942, six weeks after the Japanese bombed Pearl Harbor, and learned to walk and talk amid constant references to the War. Our family's struggles reflected the world's. Consumer goods were scarce, and our home looked bare — few rugs on the floor, flimsy home-made curtains on the windows.

My father, a journalist, wanted to go abroad as a war correspondent. His wife, with a little son and another on the way, opposed him. I don't know if the Associated Press knew anything about this, but in any case it delayed sending William Phillips to London until after the bombs and rockets stopped falling, and the family could follow him in relative safety.

By then we lived on Long Island, next to a big Catholic church, and on the day the war ended in 1945 they rang the church bells. My mother ran in from the back porch to tell me the war was over! This was a complete surprise. I was so excited that I ran out, fell off the porch and broke my collarbone, becoming possibly the first casualty of the post-war era.

A few months later, my mother, my baby brother Angus and I were sailing to England, aboard a decrepit former troop ship, the *John Erickson*. The Atlantic was still seeded with mines, so every day for eleven days we had to go through a life-saving drill. When the siren went off, we pulled on our life preservers and stood in a crowd on deck, looking out over the gray ocean. That didn't scare me much, because my mother was there, telling me about mines and lifeboats in her cheery schoolteacher manner. But I did get the fright of my life aboard the *John Erickson*. We were standing by the rail, chatting with a fellow passenger, when this man picked me up and held me over the side of the ship, apparently as a joke. I never forgot the sight of the roiling, boiling foam below, as I went rigid in the hands of this stranger.

In London, the dominant sight was ruins — the aftermath of the German blitz. Bricks and half-bricks were scattered everywhere, and buildings were gutted, with gaping holes in their sides. Bomb shelters were still intact, sandbags piled around the entrances. I remember peeking inside and imagining what it was like to spend the night underground, with bombs exploding outside.

Food was still rationed. We were allowed one egg per person per week. As a child I was eligible for a weekly glass of orange juice, which I downed at a neighborhood clinic under the eye of a public health nurse. At home, the menu was limited. Cabbage was the main course at many meals. Whale meat was a treat. Red meat was mostly available on the black market.

Still, ours felt like a happy family in England. The country's wealth of civilization more than made up for its temporary lack of amenities. My mother, an English teacher, delighted in everyone's language, the cockneys along with the aristocrats. And my father was where he wanted to be. He always regretted he hadn't been a war correspondent, but at least now he had a chance to cover the historic politics of the post-war period, as a new world emerged from the ruins.

Unfortunately, Pop wasn't much of a correspondent. He was well-informed and a good-enough writer, but so painfully shy he apparently failed to get a decent interview on his own in three years at the London bureau. My mother said the only time he ever made anything of a story was when the British government raised the price of cigarettes. She claimed credit for that — she talked to some irate smokers and gave him the quotes that made the piece.

After three years, the AP brought Pop back and gave him a desk job — editing radio newscasts. He was good at that, but after this always felt he was a failure as a journalist. Still, he did his homework, and it paid off. At his funeral years later, a colleague recalled a news conference in London, where William had generously explained some maneuver in Parliament to the British reporters. He once told me the key to journalism was "reading the spots off the *Times*." I followed in his footsteps, and for many years made a living as a non-investigative, non-aggressive newswriter and editor, whose main credential was being the only one in the newsroom who knew the difference between Slovenia, Slavonia, and Slovakia. It's all in the *Times*.

I LIKED ENGLAND. It was a perfect place to become civilized, even if the culture was not exactly your own. At school, I came under the civilizing influence of a series of lovely and not-so-lovely teachers — gentle Miss Harvey, jolly Miss Mumford, stern Mrs. Wallace, and the first crush of my life, Miss Pinkney.

Education was a no-nonsense enterprise in the London Council schools. Starting at age four we learned to read, write, add, subtract, multiply and divide, and were at it from nine to four. Classes were large but orderly, kept that way by the customs of the land, which included corporal punishment. The school's leading legend was that the headmaster "had a cane," though I never knew of him actually using it on anyone. Mr. Tapner, the headmaster, was a mild-mannered, ramrod fellow with a salt-and-pepper mustache, whose character appeared to have been shaped on the playing fields of Eton. One day he called a large group of boys out to the playground of our school, and tossed a ball in our midst. We were supposed to pass it around and fight for it, rugby-style.

— There you go, boys, he said. Practice that!

That was my only lesson from Mr. Tapner, which I politely declined, but it illustrated a violent streak in English society that popped up to frighten me in various forms, including the most brutal schoolyard bullying I ever saw. The victim of choice was the slowest boy in our class, Geoffrey Higginson. One day a half-dozen boys tied a rope around Geoffrey's waist and dragged him over the concrete, around and around the yard, until he was bleeding and wailing for mercy. Everyone was invited to join the fun, and I believe I took hold of that rope for a few seconds, though I dropped it at the sight of blood.

Inside the school, the only ones who actually hit us were the "big girls," ten or eleven-year-olds who watched the class when the teacher was out of the room. They would prowl the aisles with rulers at the ready, looking for anyone who dared speak or make a false move. One day I must have done something.

— Put out yer 'and, ordered the big girl.

I was petrified, and hid my hands behind me.

— Put out yer 'and! she insisted, but another big girl intervened.

— 'E's afraid, she said. Leave 'im alone.

It was my first offense, so I was pardoned.

For the most part I was a teacher's pet at school, possibly

because I was an American in a country that was grateful for America's help in the war, but also because I could be a cherubic little fellow in those days.

Most school days started with singing, the teacher leading the class in hymns and traditional English songs. I loved to sing, and one day I felt the music fairly bursting out of me. I opened my mouth to let it out, and while I hadn't meant to call attention to myself, Miss Mumford spotted me in full-throated ecstasy. She called me up to the desk, and in front of everyone presented me with a pretty little calendar, for singing so joyfully. After that I watched my mouth.

On the whole, I liked school. We were encouraged to read on our own, and promoted as soon as we had mastered the year's material. By the time I was seven I was in Miss Pinkney's class with nine-year-olds. I didn't have any friends among my classmates, but I loved my teacher. Miss Pinkney was tall and fair, straightforward and sweet, and met my gaze in a manner that convinced me she loved me too. On my last day of school in England she took the class out for a treat, a game of cricket in the schoolyard. She served as the bowler – the cricket equivalent of pitcher – which may have been unusual for a female in those days. This little batsman was bowled over by her blue eyes and the strong, smooth arms that swung from her short-sleeved English blouse. Thank you, Miss Pinkney, for everything.

ENGLAND WAS WHERE I MADE my first friend. I was playing on the sidewalk near Barnes Common in our London suburb, when I saw a little fair-haired boy across the street, just my size. Neither of us was allowed to cross the street, and if I'd been a proper English boy I might never have said a word. But as an American I was comfortable with shouting, and curious about this little lad.

— What's your name? I yelled across the way.

— Christopher Wigley, he replied. I thought that was hilarious.

— You mean, like a wiggly worm?

— Oh, no! Not at all.

— Can you cross the street and play?

— No, but my mum can bring me.

— Well then, get your mum.

Christopher's house soon became the first English home my family visited. His father was a doctor, Guy Wigley, and his mum was a comfy, chatty hostess named Louise, nicknamed Luly. They had a soft, deep rug on the sitting-room floor, and a red plush velvet chair. While the grownups talked, I would sit on the rug and push the nap on the velvet chair one way and then the other, just for the look and feel of it.

Christopher was quiet and bookish, and I remember very little about him, except his serene suburban home. With a little sister in the crib, a neat garden in the back, and a never-ending stream of pleasant conversation, it seemed the perfect model of a British family. Twenty years later when the Beatles sang "Penny Lane," it took me back there, "beneath the blue suburban skies." And thirty years later, I found myself on Nassau Road again, standing on the spot where I first saw Christopher. I couldn't walk away, so impulsively I crossed the street and rang the doorbell at Number Five. Luly answered, invited me in as soon as I identified myself, and resumed her stream of pleasant conversation as if we'd hardly been parted.

THE STRONGEST ATTACHMENT I MADE in London was to the river Thames. I've always been drawn to rivers, especially big rivers running through great cities, and the Thames was my first. We lived just a long block away, and I remember asking my mother nearly every day if I could walk down to see the river. I wasn't allowed to cross the main road, but a small boy could just glimpse the water from across the way. I'd stand on the corner for I don't know how long, just watching it flow. Later, when I was six and allowed to cross, I'd look out over the low wall at the tide, coming and going in the estuary. At low tide the stream narrowed, revealing wet rocks covered in moss, and cockles and mussels, alive, alive-o.

The greatest thrill of my London years came beside the river. It was the day of the boat race between Oxford and Cambridge, and we walked down to the banks of the Thames to watch. The whole neighborhood was there – butchers and bakers, barbers, fishmongers and fishwives. We all looked upriver, under the Hammersmith Bridge, waiting for them to come around the bend. Suddenly a roar went up – the first crew appeared, flashing light blue trim on their oars. Cambridge was in the lead! The Oxford crew, with dark blue tips, labored a few lengths behind. The roar built as they pulled past us, six men to a crew, rowing mightily, the coxwains barking through their megaphones, urging them on. I became a Cambridge man on the spot, and light blue has been my favorite color every since.

A CAMBRIDGE MAN, YET AN AMERICAN BOY, I was only half-civilized. My tendency to shout and call attention to myself disqualified me from polite society, though of course the British were too polite to tell me so. For example, on Guy Fawkes Day — the British equivalent of the Fourth of July — the custom was for children to parade around with an effigy of the traitor, which was then thrown on a bonfire that night. Grownups, we were told, would give you a "penny for the Guy," so Angus and I spent an afternoon on the corner with our dummy, screaming, *"Penny For The Guy!"* at every passerby. For this we received a series of tight smiles, and not one penny. Later my mother explained the English way would have been to request politely, "Sir, may I have a penny for the Guy?" That struck me as demeaning.

Yelling at people was not even my worst offense. Somehow I got it into my head that as an American, I didn't have to obey any rules, so I felt free to pull down my pants and point my rear end at little girls. This never failed to produce squeals of what I took to be delight. I don't know if my parents were aware of these exploits, but in any case they never warned me I could get into trouble for mooning.

Eventually, though, I was spanked for it, by a guest in our house. Hazel Loesch was a friend of my mother, and looked much like her, except that Hazel wore makeup, perfume, and a girdle. She had taught high-school English with my mother, and as a single woman she was able to sail to England every summer and stay with us for a short vacation.

Unlike my parents, Hazel had firm ideas about the rules of behavior in mixed company. One day when the grownups were chatting downstairs, I wandered through Hazel's guest room on the second floor, and out onto a little balcony. From there I spied a couple of school girls coming down the road.

— Look, said one. 'E's the one who pulls down 'is trousers!
— Go on, 'e don't, said the other.

Eager to correct any doubts, I whirled around, pulled down my pants and bent over. Squeals of delight arose from the sidewalk! But before I could even straighten up to acknowledge my triumph, I was seized and dragged off the balcony, and roughly turned over Hazel's knee. She spanked me at least five times, as hard as she could. I howled in pain and anger, and ran out of the room. Later she spoke to me in a calm voice.

— I didn't spank you because you were in my room, she said. I spanked you because you dropped your pants.

I knew that. What I didn't know was that it was wrong to invade a lady's room in the first place. In fact I often dropped in when she wasn't there, to visit her exotic collection of toiletries.

Hazel arranged her perfumes, powders, paint-brushes and creams in neat rows on the dressing table. The cut-glass vials in particular were like nothing I'd ever seen in our house, but more than the sights, it was the smells that lured me to her boudoir. One day I dared to open a vial of perfume, and stood there with the dropper in my hand, longing to release the liquid inside. But where to drop it? I didn't dare put it on myself, so I stole into the next room where my baby brother was sleeping.

Like a madman, I leaned over the crib and squeezed one drop of perfume right into his eye!

He winced and rolled over.

What if I've blinded him! I thought. I ran out of the room and replaced the bottle. No one had seen me, but I never felt so exposed in my life.

What was I trying to do? For years I wondered if I'd been trying to kill my brother, or turn him into a girl. But many years later I realized I was experimenting on him. What I really wanted was to turn myself into a girl, or more precisely, find a way to enter the artificial, sensuous realm that Hazel brought into our soap-and-water household.

To this day, I have never entered that realm. Woman who wear perfume fascinate me, but they scare me away. Like

Hazel, they seem to live in a world where men and women have different natures, and opposite values.

I could never put perfume on myself. In fact, I wound up delivering one more affront to British civilization by splashing myself with water from a horse-trough.

The trough was in downtown Barnes, halfway along my "marathon" route. I started running through town after Pop brought me to the 1948 Olympics at Wembley Stadium in London, where I was fascinated by the long-distance runners. Emil Zatopek of Czechoslovakia became my first hero. He won the ten thousand meters by outlasting everyone, grinding out the laps with a steady stride and gaze, while others literally fell by the wayside in the summer heat.

Eager to run my own race, I recruited the fastest boy in school to try long-distance with me. Terry Jessiman and I would take off our shirts and run about two miles through Barnes, along streets and alleys to the banks of the Thames, then parallel with the river back to my house. The cool water in the horse-trough looked irresistible to a sweaty athlete in mid-race, so I would scoop it up with both hands and dump it over my head, without breaking stride through the marketplace. Terry did the same, following my bizarre example. I remember looking up to see an English lady shrieking in dismay at the sight.

— What a horrid little boy! she seemed to say, to ignore the distinction between man and beast. This was just more upper-class English rot to me.

AMONG MY PEERS I got a reputation as a noble savage. Once I estimated the time for some fellows in the street, and one of them said knowingly:

— E's a Canadian, 'e can tell time by the sun.

We spent three years in London, until I was seven, and by then I was dying to move back to America. I thought that there I would finally get a horse.

BEING AN AMERICAN

I N THE SUMMER OF 1949 we sailed back to America, this time on the *Queen Mary*, flagship of the luxury Cunard Line. We went first class because the AP had assigned my father to "shadow" the British health minister, Aneurin Bevan, on his way to a UN meeting in New York. Pop didn't gather any news that I knew of, but the weather was beautiful — the sky bright blue, the ocean deep blue, as we spent our days strolling and lounging on the top deck of the immense liner.

Bevan, a coal miner's son who designed Britain's National Health Service, probably felt as out of place as we did. The British class system was still rigidly intact aboard the *Queen Mary*. Passengers were divided into first class, cabin class and tourist class, and they never mixed. The first-class deck had a huge swimming pool and chairs you could put anywhere you wanted. Facing the stern, we could look down at the cabin-class deck, with a smaller pool and chairs comfortably spaced in rows, and then beyond into tourist class — a tiny deck just above the engine's wake, with no pool, and chairs crammed together. It was obvious that we didn't belong up here, but years later I realized that this was one of the few perks of the journalistic trade — living like a king on the road. The *Queen Mary* prepared me to enjoy my stays in some of the world's finer hostelries, made sweeter by the knowledge that I didn't belong there.

After just four days at sea, we sailed under the Statue of Liberty and docked on the west side of Manhattan. America was my native home, but I'd been away so long that everything looked strange. I had made up a fictional version of the USA, but it bore no resemblance to the canyons of Manhattan, or the cramped suburbs of Queens we drove through on our way home to Roslyn. I spent the whole trip looking anxiously out the window for open spaces and horses, and saw none. By the time we pulled into our driveway, my dream of becoming a cowboy had been squashed down to a sliver of hope that somehow, my eyes were lying.

They weren't. Roslyn was not the city — it had woods and marshes to ramble in — but the biggest open space was the high-school playing field, and there were fewer horses than in London.

Not only did I never get a horse, I even got in trouble for drawing a horse. I drew it in school, of an everyday street scene from London. A milkman's nag was standing in the road, with a feedbag on his face and a row of turds spilling out of his bunghole into a steaming pile on the pavement. I handed it in and a few minutes later, the teacher — a sweet young lady in a smock, Miss DePaolo — called me up to the desk, and told me I had done something very bad. She then ripped up my drawing and threw it in the waste basket! I was stunned. At home that night, my mother explained that in America, some people were offended by basic animal functions. That was the strangest thing I ever heard, but only one of many adjustments I had to make to living in my native land.

I soon learned that if an American boy wanted to be quiet and bookish, he would have to do it on his own time. Social life consisted of sports, vandalism, and fighting and I had to show that I had what it takes to be one of the boys.

The neighborhood gang put up with my short pants and funny accent for about two weeks, then decided they'd been polite enough to the newcomer. One day I walked out of the house to see them sitting in a row on the culvert across the street, waiting for me.

— We dare you to fight us, said the biggest one.

I'd never been in a fight in my life, so I went back in the house and told my mother. To my surprise, she said I should go out and fight them, one at a time.

I took a breath, then grabbed a baseball bat, slung it over my shoulder and walked out the door.

— All right, I said. I'll fight you, one at a time.

They were impressed.

— OK, said the biggest one. You can use the bat and we'll just fight with bare hands.

— No, that's all right.

I chose the littlest guy as my first opponent, and promptly thrashed him. This kid's parents were friends of ours, and they'd been staying in our house while we were in England. He was supposed to be my first friend in America, and I took pleasure in paying him back for his hospitality.

After that the other boys thrashed me. The fights took a

minute or less, just long enough to establish a winner. I evidently got good marks for my willingness to take a beating, because afterwards they invited me to play "war." We spent the afternoon rambling around the neighborhood, popping up from behind bushes to annihilate each other with machine-gun sounds: *DOW DOW DOW DOW DOW DOW DOW!*

At the end of the day I felt relieved that I'd been accepted, and for the first time, a little bit rueful about being an American.

The truth was, at the age of seven I had lost my personal world and my little place in it. So I set about renegotiating the terms of my existence. I wanted to be accepted, but also wanted to set myself apart, to be more than one of the boys.

I began telling lies. I said I had rooted for the Germans in the war, an outrageous statement that was met with such genuine horror that I quickly took it back.

After that I told the neighborhood kids we were all Indians, kidnapped at birth and forced to grow up in white society. I remember sitting in the woods with two younger boys, telling them the sound of a passing train was actually the din of a battle between our tribe, the Shawnees, and the enemy Pawnees.

— It's over, I said, as the rattle died away. The Shawnees have won.

As chief, I could interpret distant sounds in great detail, but my Indian companions were only half convinced.

MY GREATEST WHOPPER, which I nearly got away with, was telling my third-grade class about my trip to Switzerland. We were assigned to give an oral report about some place we'd visited, so I came up with a word-for-word account of Miss Pinkney's vacation in the Alps, which she had described to our class in England a year earlier. We stayed in a little cottage on a mountain-side, with a Swiss family, I told my wide-eyed audience. This report was so well-received that the teacher proceeded to share it on parents' night, with a wide-eyed audience that included my mother. She didn't out me in front of everyone, but she did tell the teacher afterwards I had never been to Switzerland in my life.

Lying got me in more trouble than it was worth, but I was still able to earn distinction, up to the age of eight, by showing my naked butt. My ultimate trick was mooning the police.

I took a dare, as I often felt obliged to, and every kid in the neighborhood lined up to watch, squealing under their breath in anticipation as a police car with two cops came down the street. We were playing on a hillside. The other kids hunkered down at the top of the hill, and I went halfway down, turned around and thrust my bare ass straight at the officers! I had no idea what would happen.

The coppers rolled slowly down the street, offered no response at all to the spectacle, and turned the corner.

ONE LASTING EFFECT OF THIS PERIOD was a perverse alliance with the other side, namely the Boston Red Sox. In a neighborhood where everyone was either a Yankee or a Dodger fan, I chose to root for the hated rivals from Beantown. I paid the price almost immediately, when the Yankees took the 1949 pennant away from the Sox by beating them on the last two days of the season. I remember walking red-faced through a gantlet of merciless, hooting Yankee fans on that day, a sound that echoed again and again for the rest of the century.

I don't remember why I picked the Red Sox, but it was an appropriate choice. Their star, Ted Williams, was the ultimate individual in what was supposed to be a team sport.

Williams approached the game as a science, and he cared about only one aspect — hitting the ball. I saw him rip line drives through the infield so fast that the fielders were frozen in their shoes. I could never emulate Williams as a hitter, but I did pick up something of his attitude. By age nine I set out trying to perfect some aspect of some game.

My first project was pitching a baseball. My father had been a catcher as a kid, and he had an old mitt that was losing its stuffing. Playing catch in the back yard, he would squat and set it up as a target, and I learned the art of hitting it with a pitch. It's like Zen and the art of archery — don't aim!

I also spent weeks every summer bouncing a ball off neighborhood walls, scooping up grounders, and playing pickup games in the schoolyard until after dark. But my baseball dreams never went far. They fell victim to the Little League syndrome, which squeezed all the joy out of the game and replaced it with anxiety.

Little League came to Roslyn in 1952, courtesy of a local dad, a TV producer who wanted to make a movie and put our town on the map. On the day of the Little League tryouts, we had to perform for the cameras as well as the coaches. And we'd barely begun the season when the movie crews showed up again to shoot a simulated game. I wasn't invited to suit up for the staged event, so I spent the day wandering around, trying to get into the background. I appeared for about one second in the movie, standing forlornly on the sideline. My friend Ronnie got a close-up, by volunteering to strike out.

— Look disgusted! the director said.

A year later, the whole town turned out for the world premiere, with klieg lights in the sky over our little suburban movie house.

RONNIE DUCHNOWSKI WAS MY NEXT-DOOR NEIGHBOR, one of the seven samurai who beat me up when I arrived in the neighborhood, and he became my best friend. His father was a plumber who drank and beat the kids. We had little in common besides sports, but we played every game in its season, often just the two of us. We didn't talk much, but I can still feel the pounding of his fast-ball in my glove, his knees in my face as I tackled him in football, his fists on my ears as we mixed it up with an old pair of boxing gloves.

I loved Ronnie. He was a big, moon-faced kid who seemed to know he wasn't going far in life, and was taking his pleasure while he could in the joy of sports.

Ronnie's athletic career ended when he was sixteen. He took a job in a factory, and on his first day of work, a machine sheared two fingers off his right hand.

I went over to his house the next day, and found his mother weeping over the kitchen sink.

— How's Ronnie? I asked.

— Not too good, she sobbed.

Ronnie stayed in Roslyn and became a taxi driver at the railroad station. At fifty they made him a dispatcher, because he was too big to fit behind the wheel of a cab.

RONNIE AND I WENT TO THE LITTLE LEAGUE tryouts when we were ten, under the glare of the film crews' lights. He smacked one liner after another, but I was so nervous I couldn't touch the ball in my five swings. I got a break, though, because one of the coaches knew me from Cub Scouts. He drafted me in the final round for his major-league team, the Blue Sox. That meant I got a professional-looking pinstriped uniform, and was spared the ignominy of playing in a T-shirt for the Mudhens or some such outfit, in the minor leagues. Years later I thought it might have been better to be with the Mudhens, where I could have had a chance to pitch.

As it was, I did all right as second baseman for the Blue Sox, up until the age of twelve. My last year in Little League should have been my best, but it was my worst. I saw this happen to other twelve-year-olds. Suddenly instead of a boyish pleasure, the game became an adolescent set of problems.

To swing or not to swing? That was the question. I watched fat pitches float over the plate, paralyzed with indecision. At second base, where I had scooped up grounders like a vacuum cleaner, I began to anticipate bad hops, and flinch from the bouncing ball.

My coach delivered the *coup de grace*. As I went to bat late in one game, he roared from the sideline:

— Phillips! If you strike out one more time, I'm gonna put you up ninth!

I can still see the last pitch, a meatball down the middle of the plate. I took it, and looked pleadingly at the umpire. He gave me a gentle look through his mask.

— That'll be strike three, son.

MY LAST SEASON WAS ALSO COMPLICATED by my first job as a journalist. Pop was moonlighting as a sportswriter for the local weekly newspaper, and since I spent much of my time hanging around the Little League fields, we decided I could write a column. I called it "Little League Line Drives." A more obvious conflict of interest never presented itself to a journalist, but I tried to do a good job, scouting the league and highlighting up-

and-coming players.

My father edited my copy, so it came out looking professional, and so many people didn't realize that the Tom Phillips who wrote "Little League Line Drives" was the same kid who was striking out for the Blue Sox. One coach sent me a three-page typewritten letter, begging for recognition of his son. Another dad sent the paper his own version of the column, and they printed it. This piece went on and on with this man's pompous views, winding up with an attack on Ted Williams, who had just scandalized the sports world by spitting at the fans in Fenway Park. *Memo to Bosox' Ted Williams*, wrote the usurper of my franchise. *Remember, kids are watching.*

I wrote this jerk a letter, blasting him as "the arrogant essence of a Yankee fan," but my father wouldn't let me send it. Pop must have spoken to him, though, because a few days later I got a written apology on a Hallmark card.

BY THE END OF THE SEASON the coaches had figured out who I was, and they were so eager to curry favor with me as a journalist they disregarded my .150 batting average and elected me to the Little League All-Star team. This earned me the chance for true humiliation, in the national tournament. We won our first two games, and the coach told us we were on the road to the Little League World Series. In the third game, we were behind by a run in the late innings, when we got a runner on first with two outs.

The coach sent me in as a pinch-runner. I figured that meant I was supposed to run, so when a pitch got away from the catcher, I took off for second — hesitated — then took off again. I was out by ten feet.

We lost.

A few days later, the coach came around to collect my uniform, and he was still mad.

— If you hadn't tried to steal, maybe Scotty would have hit a homer, he offered by way of closure.

— Maybe, I said.

TWO YEARS LATER MY BROTHER MADE THE ALL-STAR TEAM, but had to quit when he complained of stomach pains and was diagnosed with an ulcer.

Meanwhile I had given up the dream of baseball glory, and turned to another Zen practice: shooting balls through a hoop.

CONFESSIONS OF A PHILO-SEMITE

B ASKETBALL, TO ME, WAS JUST ANOTHER INDIVIDUAL SPORT. I practiced the moves endlessly around the hoop Pop built in the driveway, and by the time I made the freshman team at Roslyn High School I could score, even against bigger and stronger boys.

At fourteen, in tenth grade, I was the high scorer on the junior varsity, touted by some as a future star. However, I was strictly a one-dimensional player, with no interest in anything but shooting. Passing the ball seemed to defeat the purpose of the game, and I did it only under pressure, and reluctantly. This is a good way to ensure that a high percentage of your passes will be intercepted.

Rebounding was dirty work, and I avoided it except in rare situations when I got fired up or angry. Playing defense also seemed like a losing proposition. It wasted energy, and I preferred a tacit bargain that would let the other team shoot freely if they would do the same for us. A few teams in our league played that way, and that gave me the chance to look like a superstar on a couple of occasions. But I was basically done in by my narcissism. To me, the game was a performance, the competition a flimsy plot to justify an exhibition of dazzling impromptu moves. This philosophy worked all right for three years, under losing coaches, but in my senior year we got a new coach who taught a more aggressive, team-oriented brand of basketball. Under Joe Lettera our team turned into a winner, but my stock went down, and to make it worse I sulked when he benched me. At one point he threatened to kick me off the team for my attitude. That message got through, and we wound up respecting each other, though I never did come to like or excel at his way of playing the game.

I preferred to dazzle solo, like a prima ballerina. And never was it more important to dazzle than when I looked up and saw Susan Belink in the crowd.

SUSAN (LATER SUSAN BELLING, OPERA DIVA) was the daughter of the cantor at Temple Sinai, the local reform synagogue. She was a year behind me in school, but very well-developed physically. She had jet-black hair, flashing dark eyes, a mischievous smile, and talent. Susan was a musical prodigy with a big soprano voice, trained but never affected. She was also fluent on piano, cello and guitar, and in classical, jazz and folk music. She played first cello in the school orchestra. I played first violin, right across from her, so for an hour a day I had an unobstructed view of beauty, creating beauty. Once I dreamed that I was sailing through space, heading for a heavenly mandala with her face in the center. In short this was my goddess.

My goddess, however, upset me by refusing to keep her distance. She lingered with me after orchestra practice, and we'd horse around in the pit with the piano and drums. She taught me a few expressions from her French class, e.g., *would you like a kiss?* I was mesmerized, but didn't feel up to her challenge. Susan seemed too different and dangerous, and I wasn't sure if she really liked me, or was just fooling around.

Susan had a bit of a "reputation." She went out casually with older boys, including some cynical make-out artists.

I only kissed her once. One Saturday morning a group of musicians gathered for a bus ride out to eastern Long Island, to rehearse with the regional high-school orchestra for a concert the next day. I must have been in an extraordinary mood, because I walked right up to her, and said:

— You gonna sit next to me?

— Yes! she replied, flashing her mischievous smile.

As soon as we boarded the bus she led me to the back seat, and proceeded to snuggle up. I put my arm around her, and rode all the way to Babylon in bliss.

At the end of the day, when we got back on the bus, I sat down next to somebody else. I'd had enough. But when Susan got on she howled in protest.

— Hey! You're sitting next to me!

— Aw, I said. OK.

Around sunset, she laid her head in my lap and smiled up at me. Beaming with joy, I leaned over and brushed a kiss on her lips.

My joy was short-lived. When I got home, I impulsively told my parents about this transporting experience, and they took a dim view of it. *Hmmm* and *harrumph* were my father and mother's respective comments. I went to bed in a storm of guilty feelings. I had kissed and told, and told the wrong people. And was the kiss itself *verboten*? I couldn't sleep.

The next day we got back on the same bus. I sat next to

Susan, but I was in no shape to snuggle. After the concert that night there was a dance, but I couldn't dance with her. She shrugged and went off to dance with someone else. I watched and was never so miserable in my life.

Still, we stayed friendly, and I had a sublime musical experience with her a couple of years later. The high-school chorus was performing Mendelssohn's *Elijah*, and I had a solo that just fit my voice, which had deepened into a baritone. Susan was accompanying on the piano, and we agreed on everything. Mendelssohn made it easy with his trick of effortlessly walking through the scale, painting pictures with notes and words. I exchanged a look with Susan, and we stretched out the deepest note. Then I looked into the audience and saw a woman weeping! Something was happening. Later another woman confirmed it, dragging her daughter over to me.

— You want to meet a nice boy? she said, mortifying the poor girl, who protested:

— I already know this nice boy!

An interesting fact about this one-time experience was that all the characters, except me, were Jewish: Mendelssohn, Elijah, Susan, the chorus teacher, the weeping woman, the mother and daughter. Jewish mothers, even liberals, did not ordinarily drag their daughters over to meet Christian boys. But then again, I wasn't really a Christian. I was a heathen, an agnostic, and a philo-Semite.

"PHILO-SEMITE" IS A DIRTY WORD, a fugitive word, not even acknowledged to exist in Webster's dictionary, though it's been in use for more than a hundred years. It means someone who admires and appreciates the Jewish people, their religion and culture. I never heard the word until many years later, but immediately recognized myself in it. It made me happy for about fifteen minutes, until I searched and found that it's mainly a term of distrust and derision. I was stunned to see a quote from a neighbor, whose daughter was a soccer teammate of mine, writing in a Jewish newspaper — "We must stamp out philo-Semitism wherever it rears its ugly head!" It turns out philo-Semites are widely believed to be anti-Semites in disguise, covering up their sick fascination and secret hatred of Jews.

My philo-Semitism began as an adolescent, along with the change in my home town from a sleepy village to an affluent suburb. Around that time in the 1950s, large estates were being sold off on the north shore of Long Island, and the forest bulldozed to make way for housing developments. Jewish families from New York City were moving into new neighborhoods with names like Strathmore, Nob Hill and Country Estates. My mother, normally resentful of the rich and horrified by bulldozers, approved in this case. She was the local Democratic committeewoman, and these were mostly liberal Democrats, new voters and activists who would eventually oust the Republican machine in Nassau County.

I entered junior high school in 1953 with an influx of Jewish kids from the city, who transformed the school, the town, and my life. They were nothing like the Italian and Polish working-class kids, poor blacks and middle-class WASPs who had been my classmates up to then. The atmosphere in the village was somnolent and sullen, a semi-rural pastoral existence with undertones of racism and anti-intellectualism. You learned to keep your mouth shut and avoid bullies.

Jewish kids had nothing to do with any of this. The boys were good in school and not at all ashamed of it. They liked sports, but never got into fights. They were friendly and talkative and intensely interested in sex, a subject that had never come up for me. My best friend Bruce Frishkoff made fun of my ignorance, but without too much malice, and taught me what I needed to know.

The girls were the most beautiful creatures I had ever seen, in cashmere and pearls, with delicate facial lines I would study while they were absorbed in their books or drawings. In repose, they seemed like angels. And they were as remote to me as angels. I read the message on a gold necklace — a heart pendant with a Star of David inside the heart. Not for you, buddy.

But my friend Bruce, to my surprise, invited me into his home and family life. His parents included me in excursions to the theater, art films and concerts, instructed me in Jewish customs, and fed me many fine meals. In this and other Jewish homes, I was exhilarated to find a method of child-rearing far more generous than anything I'd seen in Christendom. Catholic parents in particular seemed to regard their children as born sinners, looking for the road to hell. Raising them meant reining them in, with surveillance, threats and even beatings.

Jewish parents never beat their children, and treated them not as sinners but treasured vessels, not candidates for heaven or hell, but the parents' own posterity on earth. As such they lavished them with gifts, the most valuable being knowledge, experience, and wisdom. And I was being let in on the largess.

AT THIRTEEN, I WALKED INTO TEMPLE SINAI for the first time, for Bruce's Bar Mitzvah. During the Kaddish, I looked up to see the father of a classmate beating his breast and crying out in grief over the death of a relative. I was astonished. I had no use for religious ceremony — I had watched Catholics kneeling and mumbling prayers, and even taken a white-bread-and-grape juice communion at the local Presbyterian Church. These were dumb shows, signifying nothing to me. But this was not a show.

The next year at a confirmation service I heard another thirteen-year-old deliver a sermon, on the Book of Ruth. The sanctuary seemed to flood with light as she read Ruth's vow: "Whither thou goest I will go, where thou lodgest I will lodge: thy people shall be my people, and thy God my God." This girl was not preaching to me. But the story of the Moabite woman said the barriers to Judaism were not insurmountable, an outsider could participate and come to belong. At that moment, I was confirmed as a philo-Semite, and accepted a lifetime *koan*, or maybe a lifetime curse. Craving what was not mine, I refused to renounce it, I would find a way to possess it. But how?

As a teenage boy, my method of dealing with such a profound question was to ignore it, blunder through the requirements of teenage life, and follow my instincts. This led me to become a hanger-on in many Jewish homes, especially those of Jewish girls. I didn't choose them because they were Jewish, but inevitably they were. I didn't even know one of them was Jewish, until the day she kicked me out of the house because her family had to prepare for Passover.

And so I passed my high-school days in a daze of Judeophilia, leavened only by an equal obsession with basketball, and a continuous soundtrack of music — Bach and Haydn in orchestra and chorus, Bo Diddley and Elvis on the juke box and radio. Life didn't make much sense, but music always did, and that gave me hope that life would eventually work itself out.

MEANWHILE, MY BOYISH LIFE OF SPORTS, vandalism, and fighting was gradually being supplanted by the high-school pursuits of smoking, drinking, and making out. I did a little of each, but still clung to boyish ways, and had a final fling with vandalism in my senior year, ending in a high-speed car chase.

It happened in western New Jersey, where my friend Chris Miller's great-aunt Elsie lived alone on an old farm. She invited Chris to bring some friends out for a weekend, so he and I, and our friends Robbie Heller and Mark Meyerson, drove out in my 1937 Plymouth, a green cast-iron hulk that I bought from a neighbor for $25. We spent our time rambling around the farm and horsing around the house, casually wrecking Elsie's furniture and peace of mind. On Sunday afternoon we decided to go for a drive.

There wasn't much to see or do, until at length we spotted an abandoned railroad-car diner by the side of the road. The rotting sign read *Harvey's Diner*. It was just the place for a quartet of idle youths to spend a Sunday afternoon in spring. We climbed in through the broken windows, and casually set about removing the fixtures.

After twenty minutes or so we were just starting to unscrew the bar-stools, when we heard an engine roar and looked out to see a big, angry man emerging from a pickup truck. It was the owner of Harvey's Diner, and he wanted to know what we were doing on his property.

Nothing, we told him, and promised to leave. He glowered at us, got back in the truck and drove down the dirt road into the surrounding fields.

We meant to leave, but somehow dawdled a while to collect souvenirs from the ruin. We were just heading back to the car with our booty when Chris pointed to a cloud of dust on the dirt road. It was Harvey, and he was coming after us.

— Let's get outta here! Chris howled. He's got the deed to the ranch!

We raced to the car and piled in like bandits. I was laughing as I tried to turn on the engine. Chris jumped in the shotgun seat. Finally the engine kicked over and the Plymouth groaned into gear, hitting the road about forty yards ahead of Harvey. We could see the rage in his eyes as he hunched over the steering wheel, bearing down on our tail.

Chris leaned out the window and began shooting at the truck tires with his finger.

— Pow! Pow!

Harvey just kept coming.

I pulled out onto the freeway and into the fast lane, but Harvey stayed right behind us. How were we going to shake him?

I spotted an exit about a quarter-mile up the road, waited until the last split second, then cut from the left lane, darting between two cars and onto the exit ramp. Harvey was frozen at the wheel. The pickup flew past the exit, and we were free.

When we got back to the farm, we met a man with a spotted horse.

— Mighty fine horse yuh got there, said Chris.

All four outlaws were afraid to pet the beast.

WE WERE ACTUALLY AFRAID we might be arrested driving home to New York. I thought the police had an all-points bulletin out for my Plymouth, and was so elated when we crossed the state line that I broke into the chorus of "La Bamba" on the George Washington Bridge. They all thought this was funny, and we included it in a mock-historical account of our adventures that we wrote together. Chris decided to call it "A Treatise on Capitalism," another of his nonsensical references to grownup culture, or things he didn't understand.

Chris went off to Dartmouth and came back with epic tales of getting drunk and throwing up. A few years later he cowrote the script for the movie *Animal House*.

For the next few years after high school, the four of us would have reunions to read the treatise, but we didn't stay close friends, partly because of somebody's malicious mischief. I never found out who it was, but someone told Mark I said I "hated everything he stood for." Mark was the son of a record industry executive, headed for law school and a career in business. He was neither political nor religious, and I never thought about what he stood for, much less hated it. Nonetheless this rumor wounded him and he never quite accepted my denials.

It might have come from a girl who wanted to separate Mark from his buddies. Or it might have been a piece of leftwing disinformation, from the political struggle that was concealed in the social life of Long Island in the 1950s.

It had to be concealed. In those days you could lose your job, your freedom or in rare cases your life if you were found to have ties to the Communist Party. And while the Harvey's Diner gang was made up of ordinary middle-class Americans, some of my other friends and their families were card-carrying members of that international conspiracy.

I got my first hint of this in seventh grade, when my social-studies teacher organized a debate on the war in Indochina, and I naively signed up for the side of the French colonialists. Our position was not easy to defend, and we were under heavy fire from well-armed opponents, arguing that a takeover by the local communists would be best for the people of Vietnam and

Laos. After a few rounds of debate our side was losing badly, and one particularly knowledgeable girl was jabbing a pencil at me, smelling surrender. I wasn't ready to give up, so I reached to the bottom of my arsenal and pulled out a rhetorical grenade.

— Are you a communist? I demanded.

To my surprise, this stopped her in her tracks.

— Well, no, but. . . she mumbled.

Later the teacher said this wasn't a fair question, but it certainly was an effective one. This was 1954, the height of the McCarthy era, and I had invoked the awesome power of America to punish those "conspiring to advocate the overthrow of the United States government."

That same power came knocking at our door one day, in the form of two Midwestern-looking fellows with crew cuts. They were FBI agents, and they came to question my father about a friend, a reporter for the *New York Times*. Pop, looking grim, answered all their questions "No." He barely knew the guy, he said, and knew nothing about his politics.

That wasn't true. He and Jack Ryan had been good friends for years, and may even have gone to a Communist Party meeting together at some point. Pop went to a few meetings in the 1930s. He stopped going after he fell asleep at one, and he was such a minor presence that when another *Times* reporter, Clayton Knowles, was naming names to Congress, he left Bill Phillips out. So we survived the McCarthy era. On the day the U.S. Senate finally censured the Republican from Wisconsin, the atmosphere at our house was like the day the war ended. Only they didn't ring the church bells.

THE COMMUNISTS OF ROSLYN were a strange lot, so full of contradictions it was no wonder they were able to stay under cover. They were part of the Jewish migration to Long Island in the 1950s, a wave powered by success and money. Nonetheless they brought their anti-capitalist ideology with them. My buddy Bruce Frishkoff lived in a palatial house in the Country Estates development. His father was an accountant, and they had a two-car garage for a Packard and a Cadillac.

Still, Bruce would suggest to me in a lowered voice that things were different — and better — in the Soviet Union, where for example racial prejudice and sexual prudery were unknown. He slipped me odd books to read — *The Gadfly*, about a shadowy political activist, and *My Wild Irish Rogues* by Vivian Hallinan, wife of the radical labor lawyer Vincent Hallinan. In this memoir she related how she raised her half-dozen sons to be leaders of a new and more just society, while in her spare time amassing a fortune as a landlord and real-estate speculator. This seemed to sum up the contradictions of the communist underground in America — milking the system for all it was worth, while supposedly plotting its demise.

Although they hewed to the party line on political questions, the Frishkoffs were as complicated as any family. Louis, the father, struck me as a dedicated Marxist, trying to prepare his sons for the final conflict. Hilda was an anxious mother, not so sure she wanted to send her boys into armed struggle against the state. I don't know how I picked up this knowledge, but I used it to play a joke on her. One day when she answered the phone, I put on a guttural voice and a crude Russian accent.

— May I zbeek with Comrade Freeshkoff?

— Who?

— Comrade Freeshkoff. You know, Brruce.

— Who is this? she asked in an anxious voice.

— Mister Yanoffsky. From ze Youngstown Movement. (Bruce had told me about a labor dispute in Ohio they were hoping would galvanize the proletariat.)

— Just. . .a minute.

In the background I could hear her telling Bruce that Mr. Yanoffsky was calling. He came to the phone screaming with glee. Somehow he knew it was me. From then on, I was Mr. Yanoffsky to Hilda Z. Frishkoff of Country Estates.

Bruce went off to Oberlin College and I visited him there. He was living in a rundown rooming house off-campus with other student radicals. In the bathroom, instead of marble walls and golden fixtures, they had an old claw-foot tub with a shower curtain hanging from a hula hoop. This is more like it, I thought.

WHEN IT CAME TIME FOR ME TO CHOOSE a college, I was clueless. Then one day in a barber shop, I saw a magazine article about Brandeis College, a visionary new school founded by Jews, but open to all. A photograph showed students in an informal debate on campus, in the center a raven-haired intellectual identified as somebody Finkelstein. I stared at the picture and felt myself falling for Finkelstein, forming a resolution to go to Brandeis and make her mine.

Just about then, I began to wonder if I should take a break from philo-Semitism. I had to admit there was an undercurrent of weariness under my admiration for Jewish culture. I remember more than once being embarrassed, listening to people make fun of this or that as *goyishe*. Either they didn't know I wasn't Jewish, or didn't care.

I also felt envy, for the material plenty my friends enjoyed, and the spiritual riches of Jewish life that were denied to an outsider. A veil seemed to close around the High Holy Days as my friends took a leave of absence.

I didn't think my weariness would hold up for another four years at Brandeis, which would be far more heavily Jewish than Roslyn. So I bid my friends farewell and took off alone for Grinnell College, amid the alien corn of Iowa. And there I found a Jewish mentor, and a Jewish fiancée, but that's for our next chapter.

I took with me another lifetime *koan,* received from an old man, the grandfather of my girlfriend Marla Moes, the one who kicked me out of her house for Passover. As a high-school senior I was a naïve philosopher, and my first great discovery was the non-existence of the soul. I had examined the Catholic concept of an immortal personal essence and found it empty. I told Marla about my revelation and she apparently relayed the headline to her family — her boyfriend didn't believe in the soul!

When I met this patriarch he looked me up and down. "So," he said, "you don't believe in the soul." He smiled gently. "Well, I believe in the soul."

I was struck dumb. I had no answer because even then I knew this was not a theological or philosophical statement. It was something deeper, the kind of affirmation that can only be pronounced by a patriarch.

Today I am an old man myself, an elder in the Presbyterian Church, a follower of Jesus of Nazareth, who made the law and the prophets accessible to all. But my philo-Semitism underlies my Christianity, it's older and deeper, and nothing in this world can stamp it out.

4

HARVARD OF THE MIDWEST

G RINNELL IN 1959 WAS ONE OF THE TOP-RANKED small liberal arts colleges in the country, and my high-school guidance counselor told me not to apply, as I'd never get in with my erratic grades. I applied anyway, and to my surprise, they treated me like a prime prospect. A wealthy alumnus invited me for an interview in his office at Time, Inc. A few days later I got a note from him, saying I was definitely "admissible."

I had my doubts about the place, based on the cover of the catalogue, which showed a clean-cut fellow in a letter sweater sitting under a tree. But my first choice was Oberlin, and they put me on the waiting list, so I decided to take the invitation from Iowa. A few months later I crossed the Mississippi River on the Rock Island Railroad, with a carload of easterners bound for Grinnell.

We didn't know it but we were pioneers, the vanguard of a latter-day migration engineered by the ambitious president of Grinnell, Howard Bowen. Without announcing it, he had set out to transform Grinnell from a prestigious regional school —

the "Harvard of the Midwest," they liked to call it — to one with a national reputation.

That didn't sit too well with some of the Midwesterners, who regarded "Eastern intellectuals" with suspicion. The student establishment at Grinnell was composed of solid citizens from a world roughly bordered by Ohio to the east, Omaha to the west, Minnesota and Missouri north and south. They were busy turning themselves into lawyers, bankers, doctors, ministers, politicians, insurance executives, schoolteachers and mothers of the next great generation of respectability.

At this Harvard of the Midwest, practical knowledge was prized — economics was the favored major for men — but original thinking was considered extra-curricular. Artists and writers were tolerated, but only as a fringe group. Political radicals were kept on a reservation, a tumbledown rooming house off-campus called Bloom House. There were only about a dozen of them. Even farther off-campus, in a room of his own, lived a leering, cackling satirist, a New Yorker named Guy Gravenson, who made fun of everyone in his mimeographed newspaper, the *Grinnellian Rebellion*. He called the school the "Halfheart of the Midbest."

Enter then into this scene our wagon train of pioneers — unabashed artists and activists, shady entrepreneurs, Brooklyn Dodger fans, suburban girls with nails, a Park Avenue debutante, and a folksinger with a $12 guitar. That was me. I knew three chords in four keys, and could play most of the songs from two albums by Pete Seeger's group, the Weavers, plus a few selections from *The People's Songbook*, a gift from one of my left-wing comrades.

It wasn't long before my guitar got me into trouble, with a stunt that was the college equivalent of mooning the police —

picketing the ROTC Ball. ROTC was the Reserve Officers Training Corps, which offered U.S. military training, in uniform, to college students. About ten to twenty percent of the male students participated, for reasons I didn't understand. I thought they were ridiculous, marching around the football field and going to class in their buttoned-up grays. So when I heard they were having a formal ball in the gym, I thought this would be a perfect opportunity to make fun of them, and call attention to myself. I proposed to a few friends that we stage a "Pacifist's Ball" on the lawn outside the gym, in scruffy dress and with my guitar for a band. In my view this was strictly for laughs, but when the Bloom House crowd got wind of it, they joined the plan and it took on a more serious intent. This was to be a protest — probably the first of its kind at Grinnell.

On the night of the ball about twenty-five people gathered at Bloom House, and we made our way over to Darby Gym with picket signs saying *Ban the Bomb, Let's Get War Out of Education*, etc. We paraded in a ring, and I kept them singing a half-dozen anti-war songs. "Down by the Riverside" was the fast rousing one, and "Johnny We Hardly Knew Ye" a mournful dirge.

I expected this scene to be a minor annoyance or less to the ROTC revelers, but I was wrong. The reaction started with raised eyebrows from the dressed-up arrivals, and built to a big buzz inside the gym, until we became the centerpiece of the occasion. An hour into the dance, a little student lieutenant came out and stood at attention in the middle of our circle, with a prepared statement:

"You-Are-Ruining-Our-Evening," he began.

I whacked my guitar louder and went into another round of "Down by the Riverside."

I'm gonna lay down my sword and shield
Down by the riverside,
And stud-eee War No More!"

A few minutes later a drunken middle-aged officer came out and mocked us as "fags and philosophy majors." I danced a little circle around him, whaling my guitar even louder.

Only one couple turned back at the sight of our picket line. It was my roommate, Larry Smucker, a Mennonite from Ohio, who remembered his pacifist roots and took his date for a malted milk at the student union instead. There, he reported, a distinguished upperclassman stormed into the room, shouting:

— Do you know what those so-called intellectuals are *doing?*

As the night went on, a crowd built up outside the gym, and the focus turned from our picket line to angry debates among the spectators. The student establishment was outraged, but some of the faculty turned out to support us, and keep them from breaking our picket signs over our heads. I saw my English professor quieting a beet-faced sophomore, explaining that just because the protesters disagreed with his values didn't mean we were all perverts.

When the ball ended, the ROTC cadets and their dates emerged from the gym with a new plan of attack. They all held hands and began singing "God Bless America," trying to drown out our protest songs.

— Join 'em! cried one of the Bloom House gang. So we all sang "God Bless America." For me, it was the finishing touch to a perfect evening. For Grinnell, it was a dress rehearsal for the culture wars that were to split the campus for the next ten years.

I never wanted to choose sides. I prided myself on having friends from different groups, and as a freshman I was an athlete as well as a poet and folk-singer. But it wasn't long before the old guard at Grinnell let me know where I belonged.

Dick Young was the freshman basketball coach, known as "Killer" for his exhausting workouts. He was mainly a track coach and didn't know much about basketball, but he figured the keys to success in any sport were the same — strength, stamina and aggressiveness. He hated my hands-off style of play.

— It's pretty obvious which of you fellas have played some football, he observed acidly during a rebounding drill. He considered me a prime example of what was wrong with Eastern intellectuals, and more than once lit into me in his pep talks to the team.

— Some people, roared the Killer, some people like Phillips here, seem to think you can solve a problem just by thinkin' about it. Well, that's not what we believe. We believe you've got to *do* something about it!

What this had to do with basketball was not clear, but I got the message.

It was reinforced at the end of the season, when the varsity coach, John Pfitsch, sat the freshman down and talked at length to each of us about what we needed to work on in the off-season. I was sitting right in front of him, but he never mentioned me.

THE NEXT YEAR I DIDN'T EVEN THINK about playing basketball. By then the culture wars of the Sixties were underway at Grinnell, and there was no choice but to take sides. Our little band of Eastern pioneers from '59 was dwarfed by the 1960 contingent, a hundred hippies and hangers-on who were ready to take over the place.

The loudest and most visible was Peter Cohon — later known as Peter Coyote, the actor — who outdid me as a folksinger and performer. He boasted that he was twenty years old, and only attending Grinnell because a judge had let him out of a drug conviction if he agreed to go to college. Peter had long hair and an expensive twelve-string guitar, and was a gifted mimic. He could talk like a professor on almost any subject.

The cleverest was Terry Bisson, who outdid me as a poet and exhibitionist. Terry was a rich kid who liked to go around in a ragged T-shirt, sneakers and a Brooks Brothers suit, which he had crumpled and trampled until it looked like he'd picked it out of a garbage can. (Actually, he confessed, "My father bought it with his money.") In the winter, when he put on socks, Terry claimed he would grab two at random off the floor, and throw one back if they happened to match.

Terry never combed his hair, and it shot up from his head in tufts and patches. This was apparently the crowning offense to some of the jocks and athletic supporters in his hall. Late one night a half-dozen of them invaded his room and pulled him out of bed, held him down and sheared off his hair.

They thought this was funny, but instead it turned into a *cause celebre*. All of Grinnell was caught up in the incident, which was portrayed as everything from a harmless prank to a lynching. Black students, including the school's top athletes, broke with the student establishment and supported the victim. Terry himself cleverly stayed out of the argument over what to do with the perpetrators.

— It's outta my hands, he would say.

In the end, they were let off with a scolding. But the moral landscape had shifted. Suddenly the hippies held the high ground, and proceeded to use it for a relentless campaign against all the customs, traditions, rules and regulations of Midwestern college life. By the end of the Sixties all the rules were gone, and Grinnell became famous for events like a hunger strike for peace, and a picket line of naked women protesting a visit by Hugh Hefner of *Playboy*.

The rules didn't come down all at once, though, and I managed to get into lots of trouble breaking them. My first companion in crime was Judy Ohlbaum, from my old stomping grounds on Long Island. To me she was the loveliest of the new faces of 1960, looking a bit like Susan Belink. She even played jazz on the piano, though not very well.

I met her the first week of my sophomore year, when my New Yorker friend Peter Zwick and I were playing a joke on the newly-arrived freshman women. We got something like a canvas and splattered paint all over it, then hung it in the lobby of the freshman women's dorm. We told each passing coed it was a masterpiece by Jackson Pollock, on loan from the Museum of Modern Art. This was almost too easy. It fooled everyone but Judy, who took one look at our mess and sniffed.

— He doesn't paint like that, she said.

I was smitten on the spot by her combination of beauty, youth, and sophistication, and immediately launched a drive to overwhelm her with my good looks and the superior knowledge enjoyed by sophomores. This worked well enough, and within a few weeks we were spending long hours together in my room.

This, of course, was against the rules. Grinnell had just that year instituted coed visiting hours, allowing men and women into each others' dorm rooms on Sunday afternoons. But the door had to be open, and monitors came around to check that you had "three feet on the floor." Interestingly, there was no rule against sex at Grinnell. It was too unmentionable to ban. However, the venerable dean of women was quoted as saying all her policies were designed with one goal — "to keep men and women from lying down together."

The only way to escape this oppressive regime was to get out of town, which produced a disastrous foray to Des Moines for Judy and me. Judy's specialty was making up stories to get her way, so she made one up about doing research at the Des Moines Art Institute. This won her permission from the dean's office to stay overnight in the capital. Men didn't need permission, so I went along as research assistant, and we waltzed merrily into a rundown hotel near the Iowa state capitol building. Judy was elegantly dressed, and I was wearing a suit jacket and a T-shirt in the style of Terry Bisson.

Eager to show that I could make up stuff as readily as Judy, I signed the register *Jack Armstrong* and *Nancy Drew*, or some such fanciful names, but the desk clerk wasn't happy with this.

— You've got to register as man and wife, he said.

This was obviously just Midwestern hypocrisy, but it didn't seem to matter. I signed in as Judy's parents, Arthur and Ada, giving their address on Long Island. That satisfied the clerk, so we made our way to a gloomy room on the second floor of this cavernous dump, and tried to fix it up for our research. The only light was an unshaded bulb over the mirror, so I draped my T-shirt over it to create a more studious atmosphere. We set to work, and it seemed we had barely begun to explore the subject matter when I thought I heard a siren on the street outside. A moment later we smelled smoke. I looked up and saw smoke and flames erupting from my shirt over the light bulb.

Coughing and sneezing, I jumped up and threw a glass of water at it, while Judy ran into the bathroom, just as the Des Moines fire department burst through the door, a half-dozen guys in fire hats and rubber boots. They laughed as they extinguished our little blaze, and some of them were still chuckling as the chief delivered a short lecture on elementary principles of fire prevention.

We left right after they did. My T-shirt was ruined and the room was full of smoke, so I buttoned my jacket as best I could over my bare chest, and we slunk out into the night. Luckily, we had enough cash left for another cheap hotel a few blocks away. We returned to school the next day, thinking we'd escaped any long-term harm.

A few days later, though, Arthur Ohlbaum got a bill for $52 for smoke damage to the hotel, which confirmed his theory that I was a maniac who had to be kept away from his only child. Arthur was a plain man who had made a fortune with a company that sold mops and mop-wringers, and according to Judy he was convinced I was after his millions. He changed his will to make sure I got none of it, but in fact I had no designs on his money, and could never have married his daughter, even though we did become engaged for a few weeks. She said she was breaking up with me because I would never marry her, so a few days later I proposed, and we made up. We took another excursion to Des Moines, where this time I dropped $135 on a diamond ring, but a few days later we were fighting again.

In desperation I went to my favorite professor, Sheldon Zitner, a Renaissance scholar out of Brooklyn College. He chuckled.

"In these cases," he said, "the thing you have to decide is whether you like her."

That I could decide, but I found it almost impossible to break up with her. Her sexy manipulations had me in thrall, and when I got the diamond ring back I had to give it to a sensible friend for safekeeping. Otherwise we were sure to be re-engaged within days.

The only cure was to get out of town. So midway through my junior year I told the dean of men I was going to take a semester off, "to write." I got a map, and made plans to hitchhike to San Francisco.

5

BOUND FOR GLORY

O N A SUNNY DAY IN FEBRUARY OF 1962, I hit the road to California, or rather stuck my thumb out on Route 6, looking for a ride across the great divide. I was leaving my troubles behind, except for one little thing. To help in breaking up with Judy I had fallen in love with someone else, a fair-haired junior from Indiana named Mary Jo Dolembo, who seemed to be the exact opposite of my tormenting temptress — innocent and unaffected, though funny and bright. I promised to write her all about my adventures in the West.

I'd been dreaming about the West ever since I was a boy in England, longing to go back to an America I barely knew. When I got back, I felt stuck on Long Island. I heard the name Colorado, saw pictures of the Rocky Mountains, and began plotting to get there. At eight, I ran away from home, bringing nothing for the journey, and got less than half a mile before it sank in that I didn't know the way to Colorado. I sat down under a bridge and waited until Pop drove by and brought me home.

None of my high-school friends went farther than Ohio to college. Iowa attracted me because it was across the Mississippi, halfway to the Pacific. Now, at twenty, I was setting out to complete my pilgrimage, discover the West at last. I had a map but no route, just a direction and a destination, San Francisco.

After an hour I got my first ride, with a couple of high-school girls who took me to Newton, the next town down the road. By nightfall, I was sitting on my duffel bag next to a highway in Kansas City, playing my guitar to a stream of headlights rushing by. I couldn't get a ride, but didn't care that much. I was elated, imagining my coming triumphs as a folk-singer, and bathing in romantic reveries about Mary Jo, with whom I could now share a purely imaginary passion through the U.S. Mail.

ON THE WAY WEST, I saw amber waves of grain in Kansas, oil wells in Texas, and red clay in Oklahoma.

"How come that dirt is red?" I asked the truck driver. He'd never heard such a question.

"Why, thass just its nature," he said. "It's red dirt."

IN NEW MEXICO, we drove along massive red cliffs at dusk, past a lone Indian walking with his head hung down. Tumbleweeds were bouncing along the fence by the side of the road. I was with a carload of rough-hewn evangelists headed for a revival meeting. One of them studied my face in the twilight.

"Are you saved?"

"Yes, I am." Actually I just wanted to avoid a sermon, or an abduction.

He persisted. "When were you saved?"

"When I read Matthew," I said. I was thinking of the Sermon on the Mount.

In truth, I was going through a romantic-religious phase. Mary Jo was Catholic, and lent me a rosary, and another friend gave me a St. Christopher medal for safe travels. Later I added a Gideon Bible, shamelessly stolen from a motel. I had just two other books in my duffel bag — *On the Road* by Jack Kerouac, and Woody Guthrie's autobiography, *Bound for Glory*.

In the Arizona desert I linked up with an impoverished kid from Oklahoma, heading to California to look for work. We met in the back seat of a car, picked up separately by a pair of young women driving to Las Vegas to visit their boyfriends, who were trainees at one of the big casinos. The girls turned north and dropped us off in Kingman, Arizona. It was the middle of the night, so we decided to stick together.

Eddie said he had no money, but I had $35 and a diamond ring in reserve, so I treated to him to a share of a $2 hotel room in Kingman. The Beale Hotel was a rambling old place that looked like a set from a Western movie, with Navajo blankets hanging from the rafters in the lobby. In our ramshackle room we sat up for a while, drank a glass of free water and talked about life on the road. Mostly he just wanted to get to California, where some relatives had a farm. He offered me a white shirt out of his tin suitcase, but I declined.

In the morning we were hungry but he was probably hungrier, traveling without the benefit of cash. I wrestled with myself and the Sermon on the Mount, which clearly indicated that I should share all I had. We sat down in the Beale coffee shop and I treated him to coffee and a doughnut for thirty cents, and myself to two eggs, juice, toast and home fries for $1.25.

Feeling guilty, I offered to take second place by the side of the road.

— You stand here and hitch, I told him. When you get a ride, just tell 'em your friend is down the road, and get 'em to pick me up too.

It wasn't long before a salesman in a station wagon pulled over and Eddie climbed in. I could see them talking from about 100 yards down the road, and I figured we were on our way. I waved as the driver started and picked up speed, and was still waving as they roared past me, with Eddie staring straight ahead. He was on his way, but I was stuck in Kingman for another ten hours.

At sunset I dragged my duffel to a truck stop on the western edge of town. I'd had nothing to eat or drink since breakfast at the Beale. At the truck stop I ordered a grilled cheese sandwich and a glass of water, and looked around for someone to bum a ride from. Eventually, a rangy young guy sat down next to me at the counter. Hoping to make a friend, I stayed put. After a few minutes he asked me how far it was to Los Angeles. Whipping out a map, I showed him the distance, and then asked casually, "So, you're heading west?"

The stranger sneered. "I could see that question in your eyes."

I got the sense he would be uncomfortable rejecting me, so I humbly pressed my opening.

"I just need a ride across this desert."

He looked me up and down, suspiciously. "Are you carrying any weapons?"

"Weapons?" I was shocked, and tried to chuckle in a reassuring way. "Just a guitar." He was not amused.

"All right, I'll take you, but only because I need someone to help me stay awake."

"Sure thing!" I smiled at my deliverer, who responded with

another sneer.

"Just don't try any funny business."

I sneaked a glance at the driver as we walked out. He was over six feet, and broad-shouldered, with black eyes that shifted and glowered. He looked to be about thirty, and weighed down with some fearsome responsibility.

"Put your hands up against the truck," he ordered. "I want to make sure you're not carrying any weapons."

He frisked me, roughly and perfunctorily. He still wasn't happy. When we climbed into the driver's cab, he snarled, "Don't make any sudden movements."

The truck was huge, and unmarked. It roared as we headed out across the desert on a moonless night. "I've been up for two days, and I have to make it to the coast by morning," barked the driver. "I need you to talk to me."

"Okay!" I racked my brain for a subject, but since he had shown no interest in anything except his own fears, was hard-pressed for a conversation starter. So I asked, "How come you're so. . .uh, worried about me?"

In answer, he snapped on the overhead light and glanced down at my hands. "I told you, don't make any sudden movements."

"I didn't."

The driver turned off the light. "All right. Talk to me."

Looking down the road I saw a cluster of red, blue and green lights on the horizon. "What are those lights?" I asked, pointing.

"I don't know."

"It looks like. . .a flying saucer."

The driver snickered. "Yeah, sure, a flying saucer."

We rode in silence for ten miles. The cluster slowly spread

into individual points of color, and then I realized what we were seeing.

"Oh, it's a town. The next town."

The sign read *Yucca 16*.

ACROSS THE CALIFORNIA BORDER in Needles, we stopped at a bar. The driver ordered rum and coke — he said it kept him going. I ordered a glass of beer. As we walked back to the truck, he asked my age.

"Twenty." The sign in the bar read *No One Under 21 Served*.

"That was good," he said. "You didn't flinch."

I shrugged.

"Now, I want you to do something for me," said the driver. "There's a little office in the truck, and a sweater on the chair in there. Bring it to me, I'm getting cold."

He swung open the rear gates of the trailer. Inside were boxes piled to the ceiling, with a narrow passage in the middle. "Right through there."

Hoisting myself into the trailer I made my way toward a dim light at the end of the passage. As I went I saw a large sign on one of the boxes: *Danger Radioactive Material*. I ducked into the office, a small room with a desk and chair. It was bare and neat, but smelled musty. I grabbed a cardigan sweater from the back of the chair and hurried out.

"Here."

"Thanks." The driver shot another of his sidelong sneers. We climbed back into the cab, and rode in silence through the desert. In the dead of night began the long haul up and over the mountains, and the engine roared louder as it climbed. The driver shouted: "You're not much of a conversationalist, *are you?*"

I was out of words. "No!"

At four a.m. he dropped me off in front of a motel in Burbank, pointing toward the coastal artery a few hundred yards away. "There's the freeway!" he yelled, his contempt finally congealing into outrage. "Now get out!" I grabbed my stuff and scrambled out of the truck. It roared away.

I looked around. The road was lined with hamburger stands and gas stations, all closed. The stoplights changed in unison, but there was no traffic. The air was heavy and humid, the smell of an ocean I had yet to see. I dragged my duffel into the motel, woke up the desk clerk and took a room for $2.50.

Inside, the air seemed even heavier and wetter. I sat on the edge of the bed and tried to soothe myself as best I could. Then I fell asleep on top of the covers.

When I woke the clock said noon. A torrential rain was drumming on the motel roof. I looked out and saw water flooding the parking lot. Hungry, I dressed and left.

Across the street was a soaring plastic hamburger stand. I made my way across the intersection, wetting my shoes in the stream. Inside, the counter-girl beamed as she took my order: two 25-cent burgers and a cup of coffee. I saw lipstick, teeth, and a halo of brown hair under a paper cap with the logo of the hamburger chain. She looked at my guitar.

— You a singer?

— Yup. Folk-singer.

— You mean, like the Kingston Trio?

— Sort of.

— Where you goin?

— Frisco.

— You mean San Francisco? People out here don't say Frisco, they say San Francisco.

— 53 —

— OK, San Francisco.

She looked me over.

— You should stay here and take a screen test.

— I'm not an actor.

— Yeah, but you're good-looking. And you can sing.

— Well, maybe.

She beamed full-force.

— You could stay at my place.

— Well, no. Thanks, but I gotta be moving on.

I walked out, wobbling from a blast of wind off the Pacific, and pushed through the rain toward the freeway, next to a gutter overflowing with racing brown water. Over the freeway were two signs — straight ahead, *South San Diego* and across the road, *North San Francisco.*

I stared at the signs, struck by the symmetry, the names of saints in either direction. I could go either way. Knowing nothing about San Diego, I imagined palm trees, sunshine and naïve conventional people to the south, who might be impressed with my style. To the north I could see nothing but wind and rain. I pulled myself up, crossed the cataract and mounted the ramp to the road north.

DOWN AND OUT IN SAN FRANCISCO

L os ANGELES DIDN'T WANT TO LET ME GO. The next ride I got was with a Hollywood screenwriter who wanted me to stay the night at his home in Beverly Hills. No, thanks, I said again, I gotta be moving on. I had the feeling it was all a scam, that nothing good would ever happen in LA, this was just the way they sucked people in.

I finally escaped and rode up the coast in a beat-up car with a family of Mexican farm workers who barely spoke English. I was squeezed in the back seat with a couple of sleeping children. The *senora* gave me a gentle smile as I got out. Go in peace, my son, she seemed to say.

I got out at dawn, under a soft green hill in the greenest valley I had ever seen, the San Fernando Valley. All the names in California were of angels and saints, so I figured I'd be well taken care of.

My destination was San Francisco, named after the kindest saint of them all. But when I got there, it seemed like a hard-bitten place. After a few days in the YMCA Hotel, I found my way to a $7-a-week rooming house on Turk Street in the Tenderloin District, so named for its high concentration of hookers.

My next-door neighbor was a hooker, though I didn't know it at first. She was a tall, pale teenager with a six-month-old baby. One night I saw her at work on a street corner. She looked pretty, as if she were going to a party, with a white dress and high heels. She didn't want to say hello.

I changed a light bulb for her, and became known as a friendly fellow around the rooming house. My other next-door neighbor was a Cuban refugee named Manuel. He had found an office job, and was living on the cheap until he could pay off his employment agency fee. One day the desk clerk asked the two of us to carry something up from the bar on the ground floor. It was mid-afternoon, but when we walked in a nightclub act was underway. A Lena Horne lookalike was dancing and lip-synching a sexy song. Manuel gave me a cautionary look.

— You know that's not a girl, right?

MEANWHILE I WAS TRYING TO BREAK INTO the night-life of San Francisco myself, not in the Tenderloin but the folk-music clubs of North Beach. My first gig was in a coffee-house called the Kafana, where the performers usually outnumbered the customers. For pay, we were encouraged to eat as much as we wanted from a wheel of cheese in the kitchen.

The headline act at the Kafana was a group that had memorized the *Weavers at Carnegie Hall* record, right down to the patter between songs, which they spouted as if it were spontaneous. I was horrified. By that time I had learned a few more songs and chords, and considered myself, if not a real folksinger, at least a real phony.

There was one real folk-singer at the Kafana, an old blues-man from the south, who borrowed my guitar because it was the only one in the place with steel strings. Everyone else played nylon. I learned how to bend strings from this guy, as well as a couple of simple blues licks.

After a few nights I was sick of their cheese, so I moved on from the Kafana, which appeared to be going out of business anyway. It turned out that despite San Francisco's reputation as a hip place, the folk scene was rather thin. I found only one club in North Beach where it felt like something was happening. The Fox and the Hounds was a hole-in-the-wall coffee house on Grant Street, not far from the City Lights Bookstore. On Saturday nights they had a parade of folksingers, including Hoyt Axton, "Nick the Greek" Gravenites, and a well-traveled old guy named Pat Foster, who had been a pal of Woody Guthrie. He had a "talking blues" about bumming across the country, which I later plagiarized and turned into an epic about my own travels.

Nick the Greek was my favorite, though. He was a soft-spoken young white guy, but he had the Chicago blues sound down pat, and some funky songs, like this one:

I'd rather be sloppy drunk, baby
Anyhow, that I know. (2x)
You'd do the same thing if your baby
Ran around with Mr. So-and-So.

Hey, come over here, baby,
Bring me my half a pint. (2x)
You know when I get my whiskey
I'm gonna wreck this joint.

This he sang in a gentle, almost fuzzy voice, pronouncing "baby" like "bavy," with a rhythmic pop in his singing and guitar. I learned the words and the chords, but never had the nerve to perform it myself.

I managed to get on the bill at the Fox and the Hounds for a few Saturdays. I impressed the owner by saying I was from New York, and dropping names like Dave Van Ronk and Bob Dylan, whom I'd heard in the clubs in Greenwich Village. The performers got a cut of the receipts at the Fox, and one night I was rewarded with a crisp five-dollar bill and a smile from the owner. But it wasn't long before he decided he'd made a mistake, and invited me to leave. My first offense was singing "Cocaine Blues," a song I heard from van Ronk, on a subject I had no experience with but the club apparently did. My next and last *faux pas* was helping myself to food from the kitchen, which was against the owner's rules.

— For a guy from New York you are pretty un-cool! he snapped.

That was so true I almost wept. But instead I skulked out into the street, and found my way to a laundromat a few blocks away, where an old black guy was playing the bones and singing the blues, to an audience of two or three. I took out my guitar and joined him, and that's where I learned you can play the blues with just one chord.

— Don't change your note! cried the old man, so I just stayed on the E chord, and he sang the changes. His name was J.C. Burris. I'd never heard of him, but later I saw his name on a Folkways album of Delta blues.

The laundromat was the next-to-last stop on my folksinging tour of San Francisco. When a policeman informed me the next day that I couldn't entertain on the sidewalk outside the City Lights Bookstore, I was left without a means of generating income with my talent. By then I was almost broke.

I wasn't worried, of course, because I still had my $135 diamond ring. However, when I went to sell it on Market Street, I learned the facts of life in the diamond trade. The first jeweler claimed he saw a flaw in the stone, and offered me $25. I was insulted. But the next three saw the same flaw, and offered the same price. Finally I settled for $30 and felt lucky to get it.

Thirty dollars lasted for another week or so. I didn't want to get a job, so I decided to see if I could live for free, throwing myself at the mercy of the saints and angels.

JUST A FEW BLOCKS from my rooming house was a big Catholic church with a soup kitchen run by Franciscan monks. They fed all comers every day at eleven a.m., so I went a few times and ate with a table of itinerant characters, listening as they exchanged tips on living the hobo life in various cities. An enterprising bum named Bob tried to recruit me into his business of wiping windshields at traffic lights. He said you could use newspapers out of the trash, but that struck me as more likely to smudge the windshield than clean it.

At this point I gave in and decided to look for a job. I had some experience in restaurants, so I answered an ad for a short-order cook at a diner on Division Street. The boss looked skeptical.

— Do you have egg experience?

— Yeah, I do.

He handed me a frying pan.

— OK, give me an egg over easy.

I put some butter in the pan, melted it and cracked the egg all right. When it came time to turn it, I asked for a spatula.

— A what?

— A spatula.

He snorted.

— You don't turn an egg with a spatula. Watch this.

He took the pan and slid the egg back and forth, then scooped it into the air, where it performed a half-gainer and a belly-flop back into the sizzling butter, intact.

— Wow, I said.

— We can't use you, kid.

My face fell pleadingly. That made him mad.

— You told me you had egg experience!

Once again I slunk out into the street, and raced to the soup kitchen just in time for the daily dole. Still, my audition wasn't a waste. I had picked up one more piece of wisdom, the art of flipping an egg. I have practiced it, perfected it, and tried to pass it on to my children, all in vain.

THE NEXT DAY THE RENT WAS DUE, and I didn't have it. But I still wasn't worried, because the bums told me the church would give you a ticket to stay in a hotel. All you had to do was show up at the soup-kitchen office at five p.m., ask, and it shall be given.

The volunteer worker gave me a quizzical look when I appeared, but he did hand me a ticket good for one night at the Daton Hotel. The address was in the Mission District, the poorest part of town.

I went back to Turk Street and packed up. Manuel looked in and I told him the situation. He said he would help me carry my stuff. We walked across Market Street and found the Daton, a ten-storey building with a red neon sign on the roof. The lobby was dark and smelled musty. I gave the ticket to the desk clerk and we went upstairs.

On the fifth floor, a naked man was stumbling down the hallway with a bottle in his hand. In my room we saw a single chair, and a bed with a brown stain in the middle of a gray sheet.

After a moment of silence, Manuel said he could lend me seven dollars for another week in the rooming house.

Thanks, I said, I'll take it.

A few days of earnest job-hunting later I was hired as a bus-boy at Foster's Cafeteria, and was back on my feet.

Foster's was a busy chain of eateries all over San Francisco. My branch was on Mission Street, not far from the Daton but a different kind of establishment. It was clean, the food was decent, and the employees were well treated. As members of the California Culinary Workers union, we got overtime, two free meals a day and mandatory breaks.

I was the supply boy on the two to ten p.m. shift. My job was to make sure the servers on the front line had enough dishes and silverware. On the first day, the head office called in to check on the new employee, and I heard the boss say, "He's a very good worker." At last, I found something I was qualified to do.

Still, I couldn't please everyone. I was happy if I left the place as well supplied as I found it, but that wasn't good enough for the boss, who came in at nine p.m. She had no supply boy on the overnight, so she wanted a full complement of every-thing, enough to last until morning.

At first I tried to wave her off. She wasn't the boss of my shift, and I considered her demands excessive. But she wouldn't stop, so one day I decided to show her. I raced around from nine to ten, filling every rack and shelf.

Her response: "There's not enough tulip cups for the Jell-O." Tulip cups! I hadn't thought of that. But her attitude was outrageous. I wasn't going to give in. The next night I repeated my performance, adding tulip cups. Now, let her find something to bitch about!

She looked around, smiled, and said, "You did a very good job tonight."

THE CUSTOMERS ON MISSION STREET were mostly poor and elderly. Macaroni and cheese was the best seller, because you didn't need teeth to eat it. The place usually hummed with conversation, as most of the patrons were regulars, and they liked to sit around the tables talking politics and civic affairs. One old lady stood up and gave a screeching speech about President John F. Kennedy, calling him the greatest president since FDR.

In the paper, I read that Kennedy wanted to create a new version of Roosevelt's Public Works Administration, to provide jobs for the poor. I composed a Woody Guthrie-type ballad in praise of Kennedy and the "New PWA," but fortunately had no place to perform it. Instead I wrote it out and sent it in one of my daily missives to Mary Jo, for whom I was creating a mostly fictional account of my adventures in California.

MEANWHILE I WAS DALLYING with a slightly older woman, a waitress at Foster's who had asked me out. June Baldwin was twenty-two, an artist and a hippie before it was fashionable to be a hippie. She was always finely dressed in stuff she picked up at the Goodwill, and a waitress's pay was plenty for her. She lived in a little two-room house on the foggy side of San Francisco, past the twin peaks. One wall of her house was papered with egg cartons from Foster's, and on the other was one of her paintings, called "Revolt in the City." It was a riot of red and yellow streaks, with a shard of broken mirror in the center.

At the time she was officially Mrs. June Geer, being separated from her husband, a guy she described as a janitor with an IQ of 200. The failed marriage made her sad, and I think she decided never to try anything that serious again. She told me life was just a game, you try to enjoy it. That wasn't my philosophy. I had to get on with my plan to be famous and great at something, and with my own ideal marriage, to Mary Jo.

Trying to introduce another image, June told me about a guy she admired — a 63-year-old supply boy who played flamenco guitar.

She took me touring to Sausalito and other delightful spots in the Bay Area, and tried to cajole me into staying, but this had the opposite effect. I decided to cut it off and move on. I quit my job at Foster's, and told her I was leaving for Monterey, a place I'd read about in John Steinbeck. She said she wanted to come too, just for a day or two. I resisted but she insisted, and I gave in. Then she cried.

— I'm such a bitch, she said. I always get what I want.

I told her it was OK. We took the bus to Monterey and stayed in a little hotel on Cannery Row. We walked around town and sat by the bay, watching seals sunning themselves on the rocks. At the end we took photos of her sitting on my lap in a booth at the bus station. Then she got on the bus, and it pulled out. We never met again, though I tried to look her up more than once.

A few years later I did read her name in *The Whole Earth Catalog*, a hippie consumer guide, under a review of water beds. It said they were "good for life's little pleasures."

AFTER JUNE LEFT, it felt pointless to hang around Monterey. So I hit the road again, down the coast. I had only about $50, but felt I was now an old hand at bumming my way around the country. Grace would lead me home, or at least as far as Iowa, where Mary Jo would take care of me.

I dawdled for a few days in Los Angeles, turning down more offers for screen tests, and a singing gig in a club that turned out to be a gay bar. The guy who told me about it just wanted to find out if I was gay.

On my last night in LA, I got sloppy drunk and ran around like Mr. So-and-So. I found myself sitting on a barstool in a downtown dive, next to a young lady named Penny who was having some kind of fight with her boyfriend, over at the pool table. She too wanted to know if I was gay. (Either something had changed in my appearance and manner, or every young man in LA was assumed to be gay.) Eventually she decided I wasn't, so we kept drinking and talking — I don't remember what about, except that she had a loud voice and crude opinions. At one point we made a foray over to the pool table, where I smiled at the boyfriend as if to say I was just taking care of his baby for him, but he gave me a malevolent sneer in return.

After numerous beers the bartender said we'd had enough, so Penny and I repaired to a coffee counter in the neighborhood. There we were continuing our talk when a malevolent-looking fellow, maybe a friend of the boyfriend, walked up and tried to knock me off my stool. I swung around and put my dukes up, and managed to defend myself without getting off the stool, but suffered a small cut in the process. Penny said it was all right — wait 'til I shed blood for my country!

My assailant then walked out and apparently called the cops, because a few minutes later the LAPD showed up looking for a bleeding disorderly person. I managed to convince them I was drunk but not disorderly, and my accuser wasn't there in any case. After that I began to sober up, and somehow made it back to my cheap hotel without further damage.

The next day I was stopped again by the LAPD, and given a summons for jaywalking. It was time to get out of town.

DOWN TO ABOUT THIRTY DOLLARS AGAIN, I spent most of it on a bus ticket to Las Vegas, and figured I'd hitch from there. I lost a few of my remaining coins to a slot machine in the Las Vegas bus station.

From Las Vegas I got a ride with a trucker all the way to Vernal, Utah. Along the way we saw red rocks, carved into sculptures by natural forces. I didn't ask him how or why.

In the middle of the night in Vernal, a drunken cowboy picked me up, flopped himself in the back seat and told me to drive to Colorado. Exhausted myself, I somehow negotiated many hairpin turns in the pitch-black Rocky Mountains, and dumped him and the car off somewhere near Denver.

By the time I got to Rawlins, Wyoming, the next night, I had thirty-five cents, which I spent on a bowl of chili. Another waitress gave me a sympathetic look. Then I went behind the coffee shop and slept on a cinder pile.

I still wasn't worried, because it was only a few hundred miles in a straight shot to Grinnell. Two or three good rides would get me there in twenty-four hours.

In the morning, though, the first car that pulled over belonged to the sheriff of Carbon County, Wyoming. Sheriff C.W. Ogburn weighed in at about 300 pounds, and liked to bring the full weight of the law to bear against strangers who might pose some criminal threat. I showed him my draft card and put on my best college-boy behavior, but he wasn't impressed.

— We don't allow hitch-hikers in Rawlins, he informed me.

— Why?

— Because we've had rapes and murders, that's why.

I figured if I just got out of town, I could avoid further provoking the lawman. So I walked all the way through Rawlins, out onto the high plains, and stuck my thumb out again. The first car that came around the bend was Sheriff Ogburn's. This time he didn't waste time talking, just told me to get in the back seat. He got on the radio and announced he was "just cleanin' up the road."

He took me in and they photographed and fingerprinted me, took away my duffel bag, my guitar, and my precious rosary, which I had wound around my wrist. Then they shoved me into a jail jell about fifteen feet long and ten feet wide, with bunk beds on either side. I flung myself onto a lower bunk, cursing and crying.

I lay there for a few minutes, pounding my fist on the metal frame. Finally I looked up and saw two curious faces staring at me from the upper bunks. One was black and the other olive brown.

I acknowledged them sheepishly, embarrassed by my tantrum.

— What are you in for? said the black one.

— Hitchhiking.

— Me, too. Nineteen dollars or nineteen days, that's what you'll get.

Eddie T. Brewer from Detroit had been arrested the same way I was, except that as a person of color he did not get the courtesy of a warning from the sheriff.

Roy Sanchez was my other companion in the youth deten-
tion cell of the Carbon County Jail. He was in for 100 days for
fighting in a bar.

We were all nineteen or twenty years old, and had plenty
to talk about, mostly jobs and women. Eddie had been all over
the country, working as a busboy and a caddie. Roy was a local
guy who worked on a sheep farm. As for our troubles with the
law, Eddie considered this sort of thing an occupational hazard,
a minor annoyance. Roy was worried about becoming a habit-
ual prisoner, and vowed to stay out of bars and fights once he
got out.

My trial took place that afternoon, before a bald judge with
wire-rimmed glasses, in a bare office with an American flag
draped over the bookcase. It was Good Friday.

I was one of two defendants, along with an older black man
also charged with hitch-hiking. Sheriff Ogburn told the story
of our arrests, and we offered no defense.

The judge pronounced us guilty and sentenced us to nineteen dollars or nineteen days, as predicted.

— Can I make a phone call? I asked.

The judge told me to talk to the sheriff about that. Then he
asked the black man if he wanted to make a phone call, too.

— I don't have anyone to call, he said.

I GOT POP ON THE PHONE and he agreed to send $50 for my fine
and a bus ticket. The money took three days to work its way
through the system, and during that time Eddie and Roy and I
talked a lot. There was nothing else to do except eat three meals
a day shoved through a hole in the metal door, and look
through the bars on the eighth-floor window to the streets of

Rawlins below.

On Easter Sunday we watched the townsfolk walking to church in their suits and bonnets. From my lofty point of view they looked like a bunch of hypocrites, especially one lanky dad who reminded me of Killer Young, so I treated my cellmates to an impromptu Easter sermon. They've locked up the good people, I howled, and the bad ones are walking around free!

The next day my money came through, and I was released. Eddie and Roy asked me to buy some cigarettes for them, but unlike Jesus, I did not remember my friends when I came into my glory. I was too eager to get out of town. Sheriff Ogburn stopped me on my way out of the building, called me into his office and told me never to show my face in Rawlins again.

— Don't worry about it, I said.

A DAY LATER I WAS BACK IN GRINNELL. The first person I saw was one of my English professors, walking down the street.

— Professor! I shouted. I just got back from California!

— Oh, he said. I didn't know you were gone.

My reception was much more enthusiastic from Mary Jo and my friends, who were duly impressed with my jail tales, and my adaptation of Pat Foster's talking blues. Even one of my rivals had to admit: "You did what everybody says they want to do."

For the next year and a half, I was a big man on campus. The editor of the college paper invited me to write a column, which I used to make fun of the faculty and administration.

Brushing off our parents' advice to wait, Mary Jo and I got married the summer before our senior years, and immediately set out to start a family. What was the hurry? We didn't know it at the time, but both of us were terrified of life after graduation. We had no particular plans, and probably would have drifted for years. Both of us needed something definite, so we made up a storybook romance to hang the future on. Our honeymoon summer, working on Martha's Vineyard, was a miserable affair. I was so anxious and depressed I could barely speak. But she was the daughter of a difficult marriage herself, and her mother had taught her how to get her way without complaining. She put up with my catatonic state, and it slowly lifted.

By October, she was pregnant. We both finished up our schoolwork and graduated in January, although in the end I had to beg Coach Pfitsch to give me an unearned credit for gym, as I had neglected the requirement to take an individual sport. He offered to play me a game of badminton and give me credit if I beat him, but I knew I couldn't. Finally I persuaded him to credit me for modern dance, which I had taken up after quitting basketball. He wasn't happy about that, but wasn't quite ready to deny me a diploma, or detain me for a semester with my pregnant wife.

On our last night in Grinnell we couldn't sleep, so Mary Jo and I packed up the car and took off in the middle of the night, bound for New York.

Apparently we had stuffed too much in the front trunk of the Volkswagen. In central Illinois the latch suddenly came loose and the hood flew up against the windshield like a sail. Driving blind and fighting the wind, I managed to wrestle the car over to the side of the road, and jumped out.

It was three a.m. and the temperature was close to zero. The road was deserted. On either side were corn fields, cut down for the winter. The stubble was covered with snow. We were tired now, and wished we'd stayed home and tried to sleep. I slammed down the hood, and got back in the driver's seat. Two days later we were in New York, ready to begin a new life.

7

TOM PHILLIPS REPORTING

A S SOON AS WE ARRIVED IN NEW YORK, we parked the car on Waverly Street in the Village, and went straight to the Gaslight Café to hear Woody Guthrie's disciple, Ramblin' Jack Elliott. It was a great show. When we got back to the car, the window was smashed, the hood was open and our suitcases were gone, as well as my guitar and fiddle.

Stunned and exhausted, we drove to my parents' house on Long Island, where we spent the next few days and most of our cash repairing and replacing the damage. Then I went back to the city to look for a place to live.

We found an apartment for $75 a month on Hinsdale Street in the East New York section of Brooklyn, a neighborhood rapidly changing from a Jewish ghetto to a Black ghetto. We were the only fair-haired people around there, and a curious sight to some. One day we walked into a little fabric and sundries shop run by Orthodox Jews, with a sign that read only *M. Pinsky*. Hardly anyone shopped at Pinsky's any more. Mary Jo asked for something they had, and the black-coated son of the owner leaped up.

— You came to the right church! he said.

Another time she went in and asked for something they didn't have. The old man went into a maniacal laughing fit until she fled.

A few doors from Pinsky on New Lots Avenue was the optometrist, Carl Kugelmass. He seemed to be a competent eye doctor, but his office hadn't been cleaned or straightened up in years. To get to his examination room, you had to make your way through a narrow passage between heaps of dust-covered equipment and furniture.

These were the people left behind in the great Jewish migration to the suburbs. Just down the street from us was an old bearded man who sat on his porch, looking solemn. The sign on his fence said he was *a licensed shohet, mohel, and marriage performer.*

We lived in a second-floor apartment above our elderly landlords, Seymour and Dora Herbst. They said they were happy to have us — they'd held out against renting to Blacks or Puerto Ricans. Seymour helped Mary Jo make bookcases out of scrap lumber.

We studied natural childbirth from a book, and found a Lamaze class and a doctor at Brooklyn Hospital who would deliver our baby. Meanwhile I needed to find a job.

My first idea was to look for a gig as a folksinger in one of the Greenwich Village coffee houses, but this was emphatically nixed by my spouse. Pointing to her belly, she said: "Oh, no. You're going to get a real job."

My next notion was to be an English teacher, following the path of my mother and my college mentor, Professor Zitner, whose every class was a *tour de force* of critical wisdom and street-smart wit. Unfortunately, I had no qualifications other than my own 22-year-old wit and wisdom, and none of the schools I contacted was interested.

Pop helped me out at this point. One of his former AP colleagues was an editor at CBS News, and he lined me up for a job as a copy boy in the CBS radio newsroom. It paid $66 a week, about what I had earned as a busboy in San Francisco.

The work was similar, too. Mostly it was taking care of a clattering room full of AP, UPI and Reuters teletype machines, keeping them fed with rolls of six-ply paper, and hustling wire copy to the writers and correspondents pounding out hourly newscasts. They typed hard and fast, and got agitated as their deadlines neared.

The copy boy — or desk assistant, as they called us — also had to change typewriter ribbons, fetch office supplies and refreshments, and run messages around midtown Manhattan. I thought it was demeaning, and resented the constant demands of my many masters. I began scribbling a novel on the long subway rides to and from Brooklyn — a story about a young ballplayer, barely out of college, who breaks down under the pressure of playing in the big leagues. *Rookie*, I called it.

At work, I tried to redeem my misery with a poem, "Copy Boy."

> *They cannot bear*
> *My icy stare,*
> *My calcy brain*
> *Drives them insane.*
> *I haunt, I lurk,*
> *My shirt tail's out;*
> *I make "smart cracks,"*

I sulk, I pout.
I do not answer
Telephones;
I rest my feet,
And crack my bones.
I bring them tea
And paper clips,
I slit my eyes
And curl my lips.
I smoke, I eat,
I drink, I chew,
I burn and fume;
And wouldn't you?

Needless to say, this attitude did not impress my bosses, and the one who hired me called me in and warned me to "at least look busy." But that all changed one day in June 1964, when our daughter Jennifer was born. She wrapped her little wet hand around my finger in the delivery room, and I was suddenly motivated. Dashing off to work, the surly hippie turned into a go-getter who would volunteer for anything, and even offer ideas on how his job could be more productive. People said they had never seen anyone change so fast.

It was this burst of energy, echoed at the births of our sons Luke and Django, and followed by the awful jolt of a divorce, that propelled me from the bottom to near the top of CBS News in a little more than ten years. I took a circuitous route, though.

After a few months as a desk assistant, I talked my way into a promotion to researcher. Among other things, I was in charge of the *CBS Radio News* archives, so I spent time listening to some of the classic reports of Edward R. Murrow. I was riveted by his account of US troops liberating the Nazi concentration camp at Buchenwald. The prisoners applauded, he said, but they were so weak "it sounded like the handclapping of babies."

Murrow had departed and would soon die, but there were still some role models in the newsroom. Occasionally I got to type up transcripts of correspondents' reports, and was impressed by the way the good ones broke all the rules. Nobody wrote in "short, declarative sentences" the way we were taught in college. Diplomatic correspondent Marvin Kalb wrote long, looping sentences, but he always knew where they were going, and they came out easy to understand. Charles Kuralt wrote poetry, in prose form, every sentence crafted to sing. Even writing a humdrum news item, he would move the obligatory word "today" around in the lead sentence, finding a place where it would least break up the flow. Broadcast news copy was written for the ear, not the eye. It usually ignored standard punctuation, and instead was full of dots and dashes.

I GOT MY START AS A NEWS WRITER after a few months as researcher. One of the writers quit, and I convinced the boss to let me try out for the job. This was unheard of at CBS, where only seasoned professionals were supposed to write the news. But the office was in a chaotic state under a new boss, and I did well enough on the writing test, mimicking the style I'd picked up. They didn't give me the job, but they did let me fill in as a summer replacement. I considered myself a boy wonder, but not everyone was thrilled. I could write fast enough to bang out a ten-minute newscast in two hours, but lacked the experience and sense of history that underlies good news judgment. More than once I had to be bailed out by a busy editor on what was new and important about a story.

At the end of summer they bumped me back to researcher, and I was indignant. It was enough to make me look for another job, and I soon found one — reporter for Radio Press International, the news service of the Straus Broadcasting Company.

"So, Tom," said an amused Dallas Townsend, the veteran anchor of the CBS *World News Roundup*. "Would you say you'll be going from one great news organization to another?"

I mumbled something about being a bigger fish in a smaller puddle. I didn't get what was so funny about his question until I started work at RPI, a shoestring operation with a handful of reporters in New York and Washington, and moonlighters phoning in from around the world for five dollars a story.

That was about what they were worth. RPI's approach to the news was to churn out as much as possible, in 45-second segments, for use on its global network of second-rate radio stations. Most of it we took directly from the AP. We had a United Nations correspondent who had never been to UN headquarters, though it was just a few blocks from our office in midtown.

I had never been to the stock exchange, but I immediately became a Wall Street correspondent. All you had to do was read a fill-in-the-blanks script.

"This is the Mid-day Stock Market Report, (your name here) reporting from New York." This was followed by the Dow Jones Industrial average, the volume on the New York Stock Exchange, and the prices of a half-dozen key stocks, the same ones each day.

Mary Jo's family heard me on a Chicago radio station, and they were impressed.

My job title as reporter was mostly but not completely

phony. I did get to leave the building a few times, tape recorder in hand. Once I covered a news conference at the Waldorf-Astoria with Princess Margaret and her then-husband, Lord Snowdon, at which I experienced the ineffable emptiness of the British royal family.

— We are so *happy* to be *heah*, said the princess, speaking through a blizzard of exploding flashbulbs. Her husband, observing protocol, just sat by smiling weakly. (For the rest of my newswriting career I knew how to handle most subjects, but was always stumped by the royal Brits. I would stare at the facts, wondering what was important, but could never find anything.)

Another assignment was a news conference by Arthur Goldberg, the US ambassador to the UN, where I encountered diplomatic doubletalk. Goldberg called reporters in to express interest in a Vietnam peace initiative that the US was not interested in. This was 1966, and Lyndon Johnson was still determined to defeat the communists, or as he put it in a pep talk to the troops, "Nail that coonskin to the wall."

I had a hard time understanding what Goldberg was saying, which consisted mostly of ifs, ands and buts, but I did catch his last line, "That remains to be seen." This was the sound-bite I built my little piece around.

It turned out to be my last report for RPI. Six weeks after I started, it went out of business, bought out by its competition, UPI Radio News. R. Peter Straus himself called the staff together and told us the important thing was that the work of RPI would continue, even though most of us would be out of a job. That included me. Passed over by UPI, I jumped into the marketplace again, and immediately landed another job — newswriter for WQXR, the radio station of the *New York Times*.

At WQXR, our job was to crank out hourly newscasts, mostly based on the stories in the *Times*. The paper was well-written and we were free to plagiarize, so it wasn't hard to turn out our assembly-line product — featuring daily body-counts from Vietnam, "Great Society" proposals from the White House, plus subway strikes, water main breaks and other local headaches. After a few months it started to get tedious, but then I stumbled into a sideline as a rock and roll critic.

I hadn't followed pop music closely since high school, but I was a big fan of the Beatles, starting with their movie *A Hard Day's Night* in 1965. I never thought of writing about them, though, until they came out with *Sgt. Pepper's Lonely Hearts Club Band* in 1967. Along with millions of other Beatle fans, Mary Jo and I were stunned by the album, not just a collection of songs but a work of art, with a metaphorical theme, a progression and a climax — that astonishing crescendo that swept a world of sounds into a single note at the end.

The *Times* published a review of *Sgt. Pepper*, its first serious piece about rock and roll, but it was a disaster. Richard Goldstein, who normally wrote for the *Village Voice*, was turned off by the record. He called it an "album of special effects, dazzling but ultimately fraudulent." He said the Beatles had abandoned their rock and roll roots and gone highbrow, betraying their loyal public.

This was even dumber than the critics who had denounced Bob Dylan a few years earlier for supposedly abandoning his folk-music roots by picking up an electric guitar.

With a little help from my wife, I dashed off a piece refuting Goldstein.

I didn't think the *Times* would print it. They barely knew who I was, and they'd already run their piece, on a subject they knew little about. So I pulled a reverse on Goldstein, called up the *Village Voice* and asked the editor if they would like an alternative view to their wayward critic. A day later the *Voice* printed it, under the headline "The Beatles' Sgt. Pepper, the Album as Art Form."

The next day Mary Jo woke me up to say they were talking about me on the radio. Larry Josephson of WBAI identified me as "some guy from the *Times*."

Goldstein and I were the talk of the town for about two weeks, but I clearly had the best of the argument. It was the first piece I ever published, and it drew mail from all over the country to my tiny mailbox at WQXR. Peter Coyote wrote in from San Francisco, where he was acting with the San Francisco Mime Troupe. "Was that you?" he wondered. CBS called me up and interviewed me for *Mike Wallace at Large*. *Newsweek* ran a piece, a typical newsweekly pontification based on a few names and facts, that identified me among "a cadre of young writers who have practically invented a new branch of criticism." One morning amidst the mail I found a box of crackers, maybe a sarcastic prize from one of my colleagues, or a warning about the fragility of fame. I should have heeded it but I didn't.

I had written the piece without much thought of self-promotion. Like an irate citizen dashing off a letter to the editor, I'd just wanted to correct an egregious mistake. But in the hubbub that followed, I began to reckon how I could exploit all the attention coming my way. I called up the editor of the Arts section of the *Sunday Times*, and he offered to let me pick through the free records that were pouring into the office, and write about whatever I wanted. In 1967 the record industry was flooding the market with heavily-promoted new groups. Most of them lasted about as long in the spotlight as I did, which was three months.

In the *Sunday Times*, I wrote a series of articles about the Beatles, the Byrds, the Rolling Stones, Jefferson Airplane, Jimi Hendrix, the Mamas and the Papas, Buffalo Springfield, etc. I was the first in those pages to point out the prodigious talent of Hendrix, and the promise of Neil Young, then with the Buffalo Springfield. But I was not a well-qualified rock critic, and my flaws soon began to show. I was scrambling to catch up with a field I hadn't followed closely for years, and sometimes felt it necessary to cover the gaps in my knowledge with guesses and generalizations about stuff I hadn't even heard. At the end of 1967 the *Times* began to look for others to write about rock, and I drifted away.

I wrote a few pieces for *Rolling Stone*, then an upstart paper published irregularly in San Francisco. Jann Wenner, the editor, wrote to say he liked my stuff but wanted it to be more colorful and "inflected." By that I think he meant more hip and contemporary, but I was already trying my hardest to be hip and contemporary, so I gave up.

Still, I was hooked on all the new music coming out, so I offered my services to a bottom-of-the-line publication that would print almost anything, and pay mostly in free records. As a contributing editor to *Jazz & Pop Magazine* I got to write my ruminations on the Bee Gees, the Mothers of Invention, the Beach Boys and other personal faves. And I did a chaotic group interview with Jefferson Airplane, which the band members mostly used to make fun of me and the hapless editor of *Jazz & Pop*, Pauline Rivelli. Grace Slick was the only co-operative one. She actually seemed to like me, and I felt her preppy roots showed in her good manners.

Pauline, the editor, knew nothing about music. She was

the girlfriend of the president of ABC Records, Bob Thiele, who used *Jazz & Pop* as a front for his products. The magazine folded in the early 1970s, immediately after Bob ran off with country singer Teresa Brewer, famous for "Ricochet Romance." After that I was out of outlets for my rock-critical musings.

MEANWHILE IN 1969, budget cuts at the Times bounced me out of my day job at WQXR, and I too began to ricochet. The path of least resistance took me, via a friend's recommendation, to the chaotic newsroom of WPIX-TV, a local station that was scrambling to fend off a challenge to its license. The producer of its News at Ten was a non-journalist who got the station in trouble with faked stories, such as a reporter calling from a phone booth in the building, pretending to be covering the Soviet invasion of Czechoslovakia. Just after I got there, WPIX News hired a new boss, Bill Brown from NBC, who fired the rogue producer and set out to rehabilitate the station's image.

I came to the job with a clear warning about local TV news from Steve Steinberg, the former CBS colleague who steered me to it. "It has nothing to do with the news," he told me. "It's about whatever pictures you have."

That was all right with me. Every picture tells a story, so I went to work cutting film and writing five to ten packages a day. I cut fires, water main breaks, street fairs and stickball tournaments, news conferences and talking heads, and many furious anti-war protests, with counter-demonstrations led by the "hard-hats," working-class conservatives who supported the war in Vietnam.

At first I had no idea what I was doing in the cutting room, and left many of the best shots on the floor. But with a lesson from Bill Brown, and a few tips from the film editors, I learned the language of moving pictures. It's like music, but a sequence of images instead of notes. The rhythm comes from splitting them into long and short shots, wide shots and close-ups, just like musical phrases.

I soon grew to love working in the dark of the cutting room, especially alongside my fellow writer Elena Mannes. Elena was an aristocrat slumming at Channel Eleven, having got sick of the pretentious atmosphere at non-commercial, educational Channel Thirteen. I fancied myself a soul-mate of hers, and it was true at least in regard to the aesthetics of news film. Both of us were unhappy unless we could make it fly, and make it sing.

After a couple of years I was promoted to the job of weekend producer, which meant scraping together a half-hour of news Saturday and Sunday with the help of just one reporter, one writer, and two lazy anchormen. One Sunday Elena was the writer, and we managed to scrape together the prettiest newscast WPIX ever put on. I don't remember much of what was in it, except for a street protest over the troubles in Northern Ireland, with an old Irishman keening a lament for the dead. Elena cut the pictures, long and short, wide and close, all in time to this Irish lamentation. The rest of the show seemed to pick up a rhythm from this. Even the anchormen fell into it as they took turns reading our prose. Afterwards, people actually stayed to watch a replay. "That show didn't miss a beat," someone said.

Not only was it pretty, the show pulled a record weekend rating for WPIX, where the audience was minuscule compared to the big network-owned stations. The very next day, Bill Brown called me in and talked about making me the producer of the *News at Ten* on weekdays. Given my crude management skills — mostly throwing tantrums if people didn't co-operate — I wouldn't have lasted long in that job, which required supervising a large staff and an hour-long broadcast, five days a week. Mercifully, it never happened. A few weeks later Brown had a falling-out with management and quit. A weird new regime came in, non-journalists planning to put on a whiz-bang show with animation and special effects. Elena left for ABC, and after a few months of misery I went begging to CBS, where they hired me as news editor for their new project — a news show set in a newsroom.

Elena and I did leave a legacy at WPIX. Along with another writer, Tony van Witsen, we organized the staff into the American Newspaper Guild. It took over a year and strong stomachs; the company was continually stonewalling and threatening to put us out on strike, and we got little or no support from the other unions in the shop. But we brought a secret weapon to the bargaining table. Every time they tried to squash us we would breathe the words "license challenge." This had nothing to do with our labor dispute, but it was guaranteed to shake them up. In the end they survived the license challenge, but by then we had a contract. It covered a bargaining unit of sixteen people — writers, editors, artists and desk assistants. Many years later I checked and it had grown to nearly a hundred. I'm sure none of them had any idea who the organizers had been, but I am as satisfied with that effort as anything I've ever done in the workplace. In part it was a labor of love for my father, who died in 1967, a few years earlier. He had been a Newspaper Guild organizer in the 1930s, and lost his job at the Long Island Press because of it. This was before the National Labor Relations Act of 1935 guaranteed the right to organize.

WCBS-TV BROUGHT ME IN to help launch a new version of their Eleven O'clock Report, billed as "The Channel 2 Newsroom with Rolland Smith and Dave Marash." This was the new gimmick in local news, showing the anchors and reporters at their desks, supposedly working away and only interrupting their labors to give the audience an update on what was happening.

"I'm Rolland Smith and here's what's happening," was the opening line. This was followed mostly by a rehash of stories from the *Channel Two Six O'clock Report*, and the *CBS Evening News with Walter Cronkite*. As the late-shift editor, one of my duties was to get the word "tonight" into every story, no matter how old the news. I got my marching orders from executive producer Ron Tindiglia, who reinforced it by calling me "Tom Tonight."

Ron was one of the inventors of local TV news as we know it. His theory of news, he said, was based on the Spanish word for it — *noticias*.

"We come to work, see, and there's all these *noticias* lying around, and they're all different colors and shapes and sizes. Our job is to pin them up on a bulletin board so everyone will look. Then we tear it all down and go home!"

I could buy that, but Ron and I differed sharply on the function of the *Eleven O'clock Report*. I felt we were like the old town crier, telling people all was well so they could go to sleep in peace. Ron said it was foreplay, to get them excited before bed.

Neither of us would budge on that theoretical issue, but in practice I complied, and had fun making up titillating headlines and teases. When Elizabeth Taylor and Richard Burton broke up, Channel Two News trumpeted, "Camelot Crumbles for Liz and Dick." I made a thousand puns on Watergate, which was the lead story most nights, with the content taken directly from the Cronkite show. Ron knew little about politics, but boasted that we did more on the Watergate scandal than any other local station. "This is great for our credibility," he would say.

THE CHANNEL TWO NEWSROOM kept me laughing, at least part of the time, through the most painful year of my life. Camelot was crumbling, not just for Liz and Dick, but for another pair of would-be famous lovers — Mary Jo and me. After ten years of staying home while I went off on my adventures, she found someone else to keep her company, and made it clear she'd be happier if I'd just stay away. I resisted, I protested, we fought. In the end I wept bitterly for my three children, and accepted a ride in the family van to the Chelsea Hotel in New York.

On my first night there, a fire at four a.m. forced all the residents out of their rooms, and I found myself milling around the lobby with a crowd of artists, hookers, and crazy people. At last, I was back among my own kind. After a few weeks at the Chelsea I found an apartment nearby on 20th Street, and settled in for a long sojourn on the island of Manhattan, a new life as a divorced father, and a rock and roll ride at CBS.

8

ON MY OWN

MY THIRD-FLOOR APARTMENT ON WEST 20TH STREET looked out over the back yards of several buildings; there you could see patios, potted plants, vegetable and flower gardens, maple, elm and gingko trees, and a hawk that nested on a rooftop, preying on small beasts in the jungle below. Staring out the window, I had plenty of time to reflect on the beauty and cruelty of life, and the mess I'd made of my own.

Mary Jo and I had married too young. For each of us it was an answer to a question we didn't dare face — what are you going to do after college? Rather than look for answers in ourselves, we looked to the other to perform a miracle, to be the perfect mate. Marrying and starting a family was a bold gesture, designed to be flung in the faces of our peers, as if to say — you worry about the problems and practicalities of life, but we're too hip for that. Our love can conquer all!

As it turned out, our love barely survived its first clash with the practicalities. Mary Jo felt marooned in the wilds of Brooklyn, and depended on me for company and support, more and more as her pregnancy progressed. I hadn't counted on this. I thought my wife would bear life as my mother did, accepting it as a woman's lot to stay home and suffer while her man went off to pursue a life and a living. My mother used to sing a mournful ditty —

For men must work and women must weep.
And there's little to earn, and many to keep.

My wife, however, wanted more than that, starting with companionship from her working husband. My reaction was to try to get out of the house, away from her demands. I sang my own little ditty, to the tune of the Beatles' "I Wanna Hold Your Hand," with these words: "You're driving me in-*sane*. . . ."

We spent the ninth month in a state of high anxiety, rushing to the hospital with several false alarms. But finally the waters broke, and we were in there for real. Actual labor was much more gripping than a Lamaze training film, and while the birth was just as messy and bloody, the blood was not the issue. We watched the baby's head emerge, then suddenly the whole girl child, crying and screaming on her own. "That one didn't need any help," observed a medical student.

A day later we were driving home through Brooklyn, with Jennifer in Mary Jo's lap. The sun was beaming and the Coasters were singing "Up on the Roof" on the car radio. Our baby was sleeping, and at every stoplight we would gaze at her in wonder. She was such a perfect creation, just what we had dreamed our life together would be.

A FEW MONTHS LATER WE MOVED to Weehawken, New Jersey, just across the river from midtown Manhattan. Steve Steinberg lived there, and each of our wives was in need of a friend. But despite its convenient location, Weehawken was in some ways more isolated than East New York. The Lincoln Tunnel, built in 1947 over the protests of the townspeople, made it a five-minute bus trip to 42nd Street, an easy commute. Still, most of the locals were terrified of New York and saw no reason to go there. "It's nice to look at," one neighbor advised us.

There was no place to eat and few places to play in Weehawken, but it was cheap and safe, so we settled in, first in an apartment with a view of the Manhattan skyline, then in a house a few blocks away, with a porch and a small back yard.

My theory of marriage at this point was simple — provide a comfortable life for your wife and children, then run off and live your own life, using home as little more than a bedroom and a den. That's what my father had done, and somehow I didn't connect it with my mother's general unhappiness. (Years later, she told me she thought of him as "the little man who wasn't there.")

Mary Jo never complained much, and sometimes gave the impression she was content. Still, something was missing. The telltale sign was that both of us were constantly developing crushes on other people. In my case, they never came to anything — just gave me an incentive to go to work and flirt.

In her case, she wound up falling in love with a local guy in a rock and roll band. He and his friends would be hanging out in the living room when I came from work late at night. Eventually, Eddie moved in to stay. That roughly coincided with, and was the cause of, my removal from Weehawken, and the subject of my rueful reflections out the window on 20th Street.

Still, I found some uses for adversity. Separated from my

children, I became more conscious of them. I'd been a casual father at home, but now I had to think of ways to be with them.

Jennifer was nine, Luke seven, and Django three when I left. It wasn't hard to keep up with Jenny, as she and I were both dance fanatics. In New York I discovered the Country Dance and Song Society, which taught English and American traditional dance, and I brought Jenny to a family dance they put on in the Village. She was nervous when we walked in, but when the band started up and the caller said "Join hands and circle left," her face broke into such amazement and delight that I knew she would dance forever. Jenny became a regular at CDSS, and when she was fourteen I brought her to the New Dance Group Studio in midtown to learn ballet and jazz. A few years later she began a career as a dancer and actress that lasted more than a decade, until she married and had her own kids.

Even when she was nine, Jenny had a deep pool of maternal sympathy. Just after I moved to 20th Street she came to visit, and I told her about my Zen teacher, a "Roshi," and some things he had said that were helping me in my time of trial. A few days later I got a note, on yellow paper with a picture of a butterfly.

Dear Daddy, how are you? I want to tell you
I had a good time when I slept over your house. I
hope you don't get lonely there. I'm supposed to
be doing my homework but you come first. I would
really like to meet the Roshie, if that's the wrong
way to spell it tell me next Sunday. Those stories
you told me really make sense, like the one about

whatever happens be grateful about it. That's re-
ally true.

love

Jenny

Luke was harder to read. On the surface he seemed unperturbed by the breakup of the family. When I told the kids I was leaving, he saw that Jenny was close to tears and tried to console her. "At least it's not your mother," he said.

But he was keeping score. One day he told me, "Eddie just slept over for the sixteenth time." He must have wanted his father to return like Ulysses and reclaim his own, but it was too late for that. My Penelope didn't want me back.

Luke loved staying over at my house, and wasn't hard to entertain. A quiet fellow with technical interests, he would walk around the city counting fire hydrants or subway stations, or taking black-and-white pictures of buildings and bridges, in the style of Walker Evans. Luke has always been his own man, independent to an extreme. As a baby he would hurt Mary Jo's feelings by pushing her away when he was done nursing. He didn't need to snuggle.

Years later, when he told me how alone and miserable he felt in the years after I left, I tried to console him with a hug. But he said firmly, "I don't need a hug." I was more upset than he was, so he consoled me. "It's OK," he said. "It's my life."

It took me years to apologize to Luke. When I finally told him I was sorry, he said, "That's all I ever wanted to hear."

LITTLE DJANGO WAS THE HARDEST CASE. A week after leaving, I came back to Weehawken to visit the kids. He was playing on the sidewalk and, when he saw me, he froze in his tracks with a look of horror. I ran over, scooped him up and hugged him, and there we began a new life as father and son.

It wasn't easy, as Django barely knew who I was. He thought my name was "Morny" because when I lived at home, I would emerge from the attic late every morning — I was sleeping there, a kind of halfway house before moving out — and greet him with "Good morning!" Then I'd go off to work. Later he thought my name was Murray. He knew I wrote the news for TV, and he had me mixed up with Murray Slaughter, the TV newswriter on the *Mary Tyler Moore Show*, who looked a little like me.

When Django was four he asked to stay over at my house, like Jenny and Luke. The first time, he cried until two in the morning — he missed his mother. But the next time I saw him he said promptly, "When I come over, I won't miss Mom."

Django liked to hang out, drawing pictures and making up games. Once we made up an Olympic high-jumping event, played with a stick and a limberjack, a gangly dancing doll. The limberjack would gallop across the floor and either fall on his face or vault impossibly high over the stick. The winner was Pepperoni Pizzapants of Italy. His technique was to take a hot pizza and stuff it in his pants to make himself jump higher. This cracked Django up, and we were still talking about it the next morning. "That was funny," he said, looking to me for confirmation.

Once the bus drivers went on strike so we had to cancel a visit. "That was sad," he said.

When Django was seven I took off for India. I told the kids I'd only be gone a few months, but Django was not convinced. "Don't get a job and stay there," he pleaded. I wrote to the kids regularly from India, but when I came back, his voice was shy and faint on the phone.

I went to see him, bringing a present from India, and we took a long walk on the Weehawken waterfront, by the abandoned railroad tracks. It was a warm spring day, and finally the ice started to melt between us. I asked him what he wanted to be when he grew up. He answered, with no hesitation, "I want to be like you."

How so?

"You know. Cool."

Later it was time to catch the bus back to the city. All three kids walked me to the bus stop, but Django began squabbling with Jenny over some imaginary insult. The fight escalated and she turned away, saying he was impossible. He began crying uncontrollably. I sat him down and put my arms around him, and said I didn't like to see him like this.

"Why?" he sobbed.

I screwed up my courage. "Because I love you."

"Oh." He stopped crying.

ONE DAY HE LOOKED UP AT ME and said, "Who are you?"

Shaken, I mumbled my name, and then realized what he meant. "I'm your father."

DJANGO PUT ME ON THE GRILL REPEATEDLY. "You love Mom, right?"

Well, yes. In a way.

"Then why did you leave?" All I could say was that I didn't want to leave him, this was between me and his mother. He pushed ahead. "Are you going to marry Mom again?" No, I said, but it's going to be all right.

He looked down, with tears. "Well, it's not all right with me."

SLOWLY AND RELUCTANTLY, Django got used to the idea that he did have a father, even though his mom had another husband, and his father eventually found another wife. Amidst an epidemic of divorce in the 1970s, his school offered a workshop for children of divorced or separated parents. He told his story — he had two families, they both love him and they don't fight with each other — and this was held up as a good outcome.

I can't agree. Where children are involved, I don't think there is such a thing as a good divorce. By its nature, it's impossible for children to understand, and places an unbearable burden on them at any age.

Jennifer, though she heroically offered compassion to each of her parents, told me she felt rejected on both sides, especially after both of us remarried and had more children. She, Luke and Django, she said, were the kids who weren't in anybody's Christmas letter. After that we made sure to put them in our Christmas letter, but the point was painfully clear.

Luke was quiet, and felt forgotten. Later he told me he thought we had split up because of something he'd done. This was an incredible idea, but apparently an inevitable one in the mind of a seven-year-old boy.

Django, at three, was completely disoriented. He thought when I left, I wasn't his father any more. At the time, it would have been easier for him if I'd just disappeared. But I'm glad I didn't.

IT WAS NO ACCIDENT THAT THE BREAKUP of my marriage coincided with the steepest rise in my career fortunes. Working for CBS gave me enough income, for the first time, to even think about supporting two households. If I'd stayed at WPIX, I would have had to live on in the attic.

Besides that, the demands of work were such that I had neither the time nor the energy that would have been needed to put the family back together, if such a thing had been possible. And those demands were about to escalate, as my career hit a sudden and premature peak.

THE HOT SEAT

E VER SINCE I WAS A COPY BOY AT CBS, my ambition had been to be the editor of the *CBS Evening News.* My role model was Ed Bliss, the original editor when the broadcast became a half-hour nightly newscast in 1963. I took my inspiration from Bliss's bald head and benign face, which appeared from time to time on the broadcast as he sat at his desk just behind the anchorman, Walter Cronkite.

In the 1970s, the *Evening News with Walter Cronkite* was the leading source of news in America. Walter was named in a 1972 poll as America's "most trusted man." He earned that trust with calm, nearly flawless coverage of major events from Kennedy's assassination to landings on the moon, tumultuous political conventions, riots in the streets and the Watergate scandal. He tried to be even-handed and moderate in nearly all circumstances — and when he moved to criticize the War in Vietnam in 1968, the nation listened to him as to no other critic. Just as Ed Murrow had used his trusted voice in the fifties to discredit Senator McCarthy and his anti-communist witch hunts, Cronkite used his reporting skills and calm judgment to persuade the public that the war was unwinnable. His special report on Vietnam was the turning point for US policy, and was believed to be the key factor in President Lyndon Johnson's decision not to run for re-election in 1968.

THE *EVENING NEWS* OPERATION was next door to the radio newsroom where I'd worked in the sixties, and the atmosphere in there was bedlam. People ran in and out, screaming and panicking, but never the news editor, Ed Bliss. He didn't seem upset by what was driving everyone else crazy — whether the satellite would work, whether the president would agree to appear live, whether NBC would get him first. Based on my knowledge of editors, starting with my own father, I figured all Bliss cared about was that Cronkite should tell no untruths, the *Evening News* neglect no important developments, stories be told logically and clearly, and the language be elegant, or at least correct. My fantasy was that over the years, I would earn a reputation as an editor like Bliss, and at about forty-five, I would slip into that seat at the right hand of Cronkite, or his successor.

As it happened, I was thirty-two in 1974 when a plane crashed in South Carolina, and all the passengers were killed. Among them was John Merriman, Bliss's successor as news editor of the *Evening News*. Merriman had held the job for eight years, since Bliss retired, and that night he was eulogized on all three networks. Harry Reasoner at ABC, a former colleague, called him "the conscience of *CBS News*."

At the time I was working as the news editor for the *Eleven O'clock Report* on Channel Two, the CBS local station in New York. Our newsroom was down the hall from the *Evening News* studio, but it might as well have been on a different planet. Local news was held in low esteem at CBS, and no one had ever been promoted from Channel Two to the *Evening News*. Still, after thinking about it for a week, I went to talk with my boss at WCBS-TV, Ed Joyce, and told him about my long-held ambition. Ordinarily you wouldn't ask your boss for help in getting a job in another division, but if anyone could pull this off, it would make local news look good.

Joyce suggested I talk to John Lane, the number two producer at the *Evening News*. Joyce and Lane rode the New Haven commuter train together. His recommendation opened the door, and a week later Cronkite ushered me into his office. It was an unpretentious chamber next to the anchor set, piled to the ceiling with books, newspapers, magazines, memos and memorabilia, most prominently a bust of Winston Churchill, Cronkite's hero from his days as a World War Two reporter.

I was dazzled by the anchorman's white-haired aura, but I think it was mostly my own awe at being closeted with America's most trusted man. He was frank, saying he would give me a tryout because I wanted the job, but didn't know if he'd be able to trust someone barely half his age. He said he had someone else in mind for the job, but didn't think he'd be able to get that person.

The night before my tryout began, I couldn't sleep. I just kept thinking, Walter Cronkite, Walter Cronkite, all night. But it went all right — the first day was relatively quiet, and I got the script through on time and in good order. After a few weeks' trial they offered me the job, because it turned out I was the only person who fulfilled three requirements — I wanted it, could do it, and was willing to be grievously underpaid for it. It seemed Merriman, who was single, hadn't cared about money and just took what they gave him, a few dollars more than the union scale for editors. They wanted to give me less than that, and less than I was making at local news. I held out and finally settled for a token raise.

Several people familiar with the *Evening News* warned me against taking the job, but I brushed off their warnings about the craziness of the operation. It wasn't long before I found out what they were talking about.

AT LOCAL NEWS, I was used to plenty of free speech, a loose sense of hierarchy and numerous contributors to the mix of ideas. This came naturally to the young people I'd worked with, but it was the opposite of the system at the *Evening News*. Cronkite had designed that system himself. He'd even designed the set, with his anchor chair in the slot of a horseshoe-shaped copy desk, with writers on the rim and the editor at his side. The producers were off in an adjoining room separated by a glass partition — the "fishbowl." There they could work on the non-Cronkite portions of the show, but always subject to his veto, and with a full view of his personal court, which he referred to simply as "the desk."

If he felt things were getting out of his control, he would thunder, "Everything begins and ends at this desk!" By that he meant all editorial decisions had to go through him. In the early days of the *Evening News*, he had meant this literally. By the time I got there, the system was starting to erode.

Walter had been running things in this imperial manner for a dozen years, and he was starting to get tired. It was against his nature to give up control, but he also had a tragic flaw — he liked to enjoy life. By the time I showed up, the old man — or the general, as some called him — was taking long lunches, and marathon vacations on his beloved yacht. He usually didn't show up at the anchor desk until late afternoon. Still, it was his show — the title was *The CBS Evening News with Walter Cronkite*, and he was officially the managing editor — and he would explode if he came in and felt some important story wasn't being covered right. Walter had two conflicting desires — he wanted a show that would run itself, but strictly according to his wishes. What he needed were trusted lieutenants who would know his wishes instinctively and carry them out even in his absence.

John Merriman was a trusted lieutenant, but he died. He was survived by many legends related by veterans on the show, stories that pointed to a close bond with the old man, and mutual respect. They said he rarely opposed Walter, but on the few occasions he did, he was able to prevail. One night, the story went, Walter wanted to say something Merriman didn't want him to say. They couldn't agree. Merriman threatened to quit if he said it, but Walter was determined. When the red light flashed on and Walter began to speak into the air, Merriman stood next to the anchor seat, just off-camera, glowering at the man with his fists clenched.

Whatever it was, Walter didn't say it.

IN MY ARROGANT WAY, I thought I inherited the role of "conscience of CBS News" along with the title of editor, but Cronkite quickly made it clear while he would rely on me to take care of the details, he wasn't going to defer to my judgment on any important questions. My job, it seemed, was just like everyone else's — to do what the general would want.

I found this maddening. As the news editor I had to make out the lineup, and have the script in order for the anchorman to read, whenever he might show up. But I had to perform these duties in a straitjacket. First, I was not supposed to use my own judgment about the value of any story. The only criterion was whether "Walter would want it." The other sleeve in the straitjacket was that I was not supposed to edit the copy! The senior writers, Charlie West and Sandy Polster, considered themselves from long habit to be working directly for Cronkite, and they dumped their stories into a bin on his desk. The editor wasn't supposed to touch them until they had been approved, edited or rewritten by the boss, which in effect meant in the last frenzied minutes before air time.

As an editor I couldn't tolerate this, but I didn't dare change the system without a mandate from the managing editor. So I developed a technique of sidling up to the anchor desk and craning my neck around to read the stuff in his bin. If I spotted any errors, I'd bring them to the writers' attention.

The system was frustrating all around, but worked well enough to keep the *CBS Evening News* the pre-eminent news broadcast of the 1970s. Part of it was the high quality of the staff, and the worldwide resources of CBS News, which in those days were unsurpassed. But much of it was the standard set by Cronkite himself. He was the most aggressive and inquisitive reporter in the business, unwilling to be beaten on any important story, or let any question in his own mind go unanswered.

One day he came in steaming over a speech by Secretary of State Henry Kissinger, in which Kissinger seemed to suggest a shift in US foreign policy. In his worldly way, Kissinger was arguing that while American democratic ideals were the guiding light for our actions abroad, sometimes they might have to be sacrificed to strategic concerns. This was anathema to Walter, a World War Two reporter who still believed in America's mission to lead and save the world. He wouldn't rest until he had nailed Kissinger on it. So he commandeered the world's most famous diplomat for a two-way interview by satellite, and grilled him for forty-five minutes on what he meant by what he said.

Kissinger was unflappable and stayed out of trouble. But after the chat, he gave his bulldog questioner a pat on the head. "That was very good, Walter," he said. "You picked up every ambiguity in my *zbeech.*"

In this and innumerable other instances, Cronkite set the tone. The *CBS Evening News* would not stand by and let the powerful and rich run the world — we would needle them and probe them, investigate them, find out what they meant by what they said and hold them accountable.

I had never seen this kind of global civic journalism in action before, and I wasn't up to Walter's standard. He accused me several times of having a "defeatist attitude" in not pursuing questions, and he was right.

I never would have thought, as he did, one day in 1977 when Egypt's president Anwar Sadat said he would be willing to meet with Israeli prime minister Menachem Begin, that CBS News should take this offer directly to Begin and demand a response. Sadat made the comment in an interview with a minor correspondent on the *CBS Morning News*, which few people watched, and he was generally regarded as a glib and empty talker. Only Walter could smell the potential for a breakthrough in the Middle East, and he came in that day waving his arms.

"Did you hear what Sadat *said?*"

In fact, Sadat had been trying for months to open direct

talks with Israel, but ordinary diplomacy had been unable to bridge the gap. With a wake-up call from the general, CBS News went into action, and Walter went to work, whipsawing the question from Sadat to Begin and back again, and by the time the *Evening News* went on that night, the two were essentially in agreement. The stage was set for Sadat's visit to Jerusalem, the Camp David accords, and eventually a peace treaty between Israel and Egypt, which was followed but not destroyed by the assassination of Sadat.

The *Times* called it "Cronkite Diplomacy," and it was impressive. Still, I was even more impressed by the one-day whirlwind Walter pulled off the next year, when Begin went to Egypt. He began his day reporting from Cairo, and no one expected he would be back in New York to anchor his show the same night. But Walter, as usual, was one step ahead of everyone. That day also happened to be the inaugural flight of the Concorde supersonic airliner from Paris to New York. Walter finished his reporting in Cairo, jumped on a plane to Paris and elbowed his way onto the Concorde. Less than four hours later, he was sliding into his anchor seat at the usual time, a little sleepy and burping from the Concorde cuisine. But right where he wanted to be, always at the center.

CRONKITE'S TAKE-CHARGE ATTITUDE was also his chief flaw, because sometimes it outran his judgment. As the most trusted man in the world's most powerful nation, he fretted constantly that things would get out of control and come crashing down, unless he was personally on the ramparts, watching.

This applied equally to the workplace and the world. At CBS, he was troubled by the profusion of producers and others who supposedly worked for him, but didn't always share his thinking. Sometimes he couldn't get his points across, no matter how he stormed. One evening he was slumped in his anchor chair after a trying day, and let loose with this thunderbolt: "People used to be smart, but now I'm the only one. Everyone else is dumb, dumb, dumb!" He looked over at me, with a hapless expression that seemed to say, *I know I'm wrong about this, but I can't help thinking it. What's wrong with the world? What's wrong with me?*

I couldn't help him. I had the feeling I was partly included in his category of "smart" people, holdovers from a more enlightened age, but only partly.

In the world at large, Walter had a constant fear of things running out or decaying beyond repair. How much oil do we have left? Can the world be saved? These were actual questions he mobilized the global resources of CBS News to address, but no definitive answers were reached, to his dismay.

One day he came in convinced he had spotted the first sign of an apocalypse, in a wire-service story about Mason jars. It was harvest time, and that year there was a shortage of the rubber rings to make the jars airtight. Because of this, the story said, thousands of families would be unable to preserve their homegrown fruits and vegetables over the winter. Tons of food would rot in the fields.

To most of us this seemed like a minor setback, but to Walter it was much more. He charged into the fishbowl, waving the wire copy at the executive producer, Bud Benjamin.

"Did you see this? We've got to get right on this!" Cronkite wanted a special report as soon as possible, before the competition got to it. He became more and more agitated as he talked, sensing that no one shared his sense of alarm. He demanded to know why some officials couldn't find an unused factory — say, an idled auto plant — and convert it to start turning out those rubber rings. The nation, he said, was paralyzed by its own technological progress, and its lack of will.

"Goddamn it!" he finally exploded. "It's the collapse of civilization!"

Benjamin was a grandfatherly type who had come over from running the CBS documentary unit. He was technically Walter's boss, but in practice usually complied with his wishes. This time, though, the managing editor seemed to be off on his own. Still, Cronkite pressed his point. "What about it, Bud?"

Benjamin whacked the bowl of his pipe against his palm. Everyone looked at him.

"I'll think about it, Walter."

Cronkite crumpled the story in his hand and spun out the door.

SOCIALLY, WALTER WAS A SHY PERSON, not at all like his avuncular on-air persona. Like most very famous people, he became wary of casual contacts, and weary of constant attention from people who just wanted to meet him or bask in his presence, no matter how little they knew about what he did. Once he ran to the toilet a few minutes before air time, and reported this exchange with a security guard at the urinal.

"Hey, aren't you Walter Cronkite?"

"Well, yes."

"Wow. I've seen all your movies."

When it came to personal relationships, Walter liked things uncomplicated. At his Christmas party in 1974, just after he hired me, he inquired where my wife was. I said I was separated from my wife. His face contorted, and he pounded a fist into his hand. "Why do people do things like that?" he cried.

I LASTED NEARLY TWO AND A HALF YEARS as Cronkite's editor, but he never did come to trust me. I was too attached to my own views. As a young man, I should have tried to play the role of acolyte to the high priest, but that wasn't my way. Instead I insisted on competing with him, and interrupting his train of thought. It was many years before I learned how to keep my mouth shut at work.

When Cronkite finally did fire me, he let me in on the full story. The man he had wanted when Merriman died was Lee Townsend, a *CBS Morning News* executive and former editor of the *New York World-Telegram*. It was a perfect match. Besides coming from Walter's own world of print journalism, Townsend was in his fifties, and had a mild personality that wouldn't clash with the anchorman's fiery exhalations.

Walter couldn't get Townsend then because the company considered his salary too high for the job. Merriman had done it for much less. Walter settled for me, but with the idea that if I didn't work out, he could make a stronger pitch for his preferred choice.

So I didn't work out.

Walter and I parted on friendly terms, with some halting expressions of thanks on both sides. He came out of it with the editor he'd wanted all along, and I came out with a sparkling top line on my resume, and the promise of a good reference from the most trusted man in America.

I figured I could parlay that into some sort of gainful employment. But I was exhausted after more than two years on the hot seat, and itching for another adventure.

I decided to set out for India, in search of absolute truth.

PART TWO

10

THE FLAW IN ZEN

G IVEN A CHOICE between relative or absolute truth, the lazy student will be attracted to the absolute. Relative truth — the arts and sciences we learn in school — goes on and on. It contradicts itself, changes with the times, spawns new fields of study and occupies so much territory that no human could master more than a small fraction of it. Absolute, timeless truth, on the other hand, could be summarized on a thumbnail, and changes only in its applications, never in essence.

At least, that's what the lazy student thinks. But why should he be right about this when he's wrong about everything else? Why should Heaven be a poorer place than Earth?

In Buddhism, there are hundreds of heavens. Could it be that new heavens are created every moment, and changing every instant? Could there be as many heavens as minds to create or comprehend them? Or is it all one?

I don't know, but the point is absolute truth is as openended as relative truth. You can learn something about it if you're willing to study, but anyone who thinks he's mastered it is a fool.

I HAD MY FIRST HINT OF IT at age twelve. At the time I was pursuing physical fitness, out of a vain need to beef up my 98-pound weakling frame. Among my sources was a book on Hatha Yoga, picked up at the town library on my way home from school.

I tried some of the breathing exercises in my room, ending with *Nadi Shodhana,* the alternate-nostril breath. As I sat cross-legged, eyes closed, my breaths became longer, more measured and gentle. This went on for several minutes.

As soon as I opened my eyes, I noticed my room was a mess. Clothes were thrown over the chair, drawers were open, the bed unmade, papers scattered on the desk. I stood up and put everything in order. A minute later, this struck me as unprecedented. I never straightened up my room except under duress. My mother nagged and railed, but I ignored her unless she came up with some coercion. It was a matter of principle — boys don't like to clean their rooms, and I was fiercely attached to my boyhood. Why had I broken my vows, betrayed my values?

The answer hit me — it was the breathing exercises! I returned the book to the library, and didn't try yoga again for fifteen years.

WHEN I DID, IN MY LATE TWENTIES, my life had become a mess — too much work and not enough sleep, too many drinks and cigarettes, an unkempt marriage, inattention to children. An occasional class at the Integral Yoga Institute on 13th Street helped me breathe easier, and be more mindful of myself and others. But it was a short-lived effect.

Looking for something deeper, I read Hindu and Taoist scriptures, all pointing toward a mysterious inner self that stood apart from desire and frustration. I cultivated this inner self, even wrote the first draft of a memoir in which I described him as Mr. I.S., the calm essence hidden inside a distressed personality. He could be summoned with breathing exercises, but I didn't know if I could trust him. Wasn't he too just a passing phenomenon? I remembered my first philosophical insight as a teenager — the non-existence of the soul.

By this time, I knew there was a religion and philosophy based on the non-existence of the soul, the impermanence of all things. This was Buddhism, and I was a little scared of it. "The Supreme Doctrine," as one paperback called it, seemed far more subtle and austere than the feel-good discipline of Hatha Yoga. But I suspected it was also more durable.

After years of reading, I came to believe Zen meditation offered the most direct path to my goal. At first I thought I'd have to go to Japan to practice it. Then I learned there was a Japanese Zen center right in Manhattan. (Just to live in New York is to travel.) So one evening after work, I made my way to the New York Zendo, to begin an adventure of the mind.

The Zendo was a Japanese-style fortress with a rock garden on East 67th Street. As soon as I walked through the door I could tell things were going to happen. The silence was so deep it felt like it was coming from a cavern under the sea. Beginners were pointed to one of the cushions on a long tatami mat, where we sat in a row with a thousand thoughts clashing in our heads.

What am I supposed to do? How long will this go on? What is it? Do I like it?

Then someone would ring a bell and we'd stagger to our feet, and bow, and walk around in a line, and sit again. By the end of the first evening I realized the thoughts clashing in my head were not a distraction, but the object of meditation itself.

Soen Nakagawa Roshi, my teacher, said he had a lifetime *koan* — a question that could never be exhausted: "What is this?"

SOEN'S PROTÉGÉ, EIDO TAI SHIMANO, was the abbot of the New York Zendo, which he laughingly called a "concentration camp." This was partly a reference to the first task of Zen meditation, to concentrate the mind. But it also referred to his unrepentant Japanese imperialism.

Eido was a brilliant young monk with a dictatorial air, and a muscular build like a karate fighter. According to him, Americans didn't know how to behave — the US was "like a desert" — and could only learn through years of instruction in Japanese rituals and Zen practice. With his black robe and shaved head, he floated past our line of meditators with a polished stick — the *kyosaku* — to whack the shoulders of the lazy ones.

Eido's teacher Soen, who would blow in irregularly from Japan, was kinder. He saw Americans as the next generation of Zen students — the *dharma* coming to the West. Our very lack of history and refinement meant we had a Zen mind, a beginner's mind. Knowing nothing, we were wide open to sudden enlightenment, the stock in trade of Rinzai Zen.

To help us reach that goal, Soen and Eido made up simple *koans* for Americans. After two years of sitting, counting my breath and concentrating on monosyllables, I got my *koan:*
"What is my true nature?"
I worked at this riddle for one year, waking and sleeping.

Zen practice absorbed me so fully that it turned out to be the last straw in my marriage to Mary Jo. It was late at night on a Zen retreat when the thought first occurred to me that she was with someone else. It hit me hard, but I deliberately shrugged it off. I felt I had something more important to do.

I moved into the attic in Weehawken, which was also my meditation room. There I slept alone and woke up every morning with a single word tearing through my head — "God." That may have been an effect of concentrating my unconscious mind on the question of my true nature. But it wasn't an acceptable Zen answer.

I DIDN'T EVEN TRY TO ANSWER the riddle for a year, until the spring of 1974, when Soen and Eido took us for a week-long retreat in the Catskills. These *sesshins* are designed specifically to force students into enlightenment, or *kensho*, which means "seeing within." You sit in meditation for twelve hours a day, eat meals in silence, bow and chant, and once or twice a day have a private audience with the master.

Soen's technique in these interviews, or *dokusan,* was to encourage seekers by laughing amiably at their agonies. By the second day, my legs were screaming from the pain of sitting cross-legged, and I was convinced I didn't have any true nature, I was nothing but an empty husk. I sat with an actual sensation of the wind blowing through me.

Soen laughed. "Very good condition," he said. "One more step." He rang his little bell for the next seeker.

One more step took three more days.

My mind soon reached a state of frustration, casting around wildly for an answer. I knew I had to get it, or be consigned to the miserable ranks of Zen dunces. But every guess ran up against a blank wall and a laugh from Soen. In his oddball English, he told me that was fine.

"You must become desperated," he said.

At these retreats Soen and Eido would play good cop and bad cop. Eido was the enforcer, keeping the meditation hall quiet and making sure we never relaxed. At supper, he warned us to pay attention as we chewed our rice. This, he said, was Zen practice.

Here was a hint. I'd noticed that while I was racking my brains for an answer, I was in a fog and ate mindlessly. After Eido said that, I tried chewing and paying attention, and it dawned on me that if this was Zen practice, it must have something to do with the answer to my *koan*. I formulated a clue: "The key to my true nature is in the present moment."

Two days later, time was starting to run out and I had gotten no further. I repeated my sentence for the millionth time, and this time it struck me as a little bulky.

I went over it word by word. "The key to my true nature is in the present moment."

Well, let's forget "the key to." We're not looking for the key, we're looking for the thing itself.

OK. "My true nature is in the present moment."

Do we really need that "in?"

Pow.

"My true nature *is* the present moment."

I was facing a window, with snow outside, and the outside suddenly leaped in. I gasped and shuddered on my cushion.

I was enlightened by editing.

AT THE NEXT DOKUSAN, I rang the bell like a fireman and raced up the stairs to Soen's chamber to tell him. He laughed.

"Very good," he said. Then he made me illustrate it with some Zen examples, such as "My true nature is trees on Dai Bosatsu Mountain." You could see the mountain, which he had renamed "Great Bodhisattva," through the window past his head.

This was the answer! But what was it? "No need give it a name," said Soen.

At the next *dokusan,* I tore up the stairs again, but Soen sent me back and told me to walk. "Now is not the time to be in a great hurry," he said. Calm down and meditate on it.

I did, for years. This was enlightenment, but it's not to be confused with Nirvana, or the cessation of suffering. It's just the first step in seeing things as they are. In Western terms, it's the insight that underlies modern philosophy and psychology — the world we live in is not one of objective facts, but of phenomena, conditioned by the mind.

I also came to understand that each person's enlightenment is conditioned by personality. One of the reasons I hit it off with Soen was that both of us were far-sighted — we preferred the infinite aesthetic distance to close-up intimacy. When he asked me for an example of my true nature in the present moment, I chose the mountain across the lake, though I could just as well have looked into his eyes. That wasn't my style, or his. Both of us tended to keep our distance, and we paid for it in our personal lives.

SOEN WAS OUT THE WINDOW even by the zany standards of Zen masters. When he was a young monk he had tried meditating in a treetop, and was almost killed when a gust of wind blew him out. He suffered a broken skull that left him with serious headaches for the rest of his life, but it didn't cure him of his affinity for heights. When he first came to America in the late fifties, he had led a retreat at a house on the cliffs by the Hudson River. A student looked out at dawn to see Soen sitting cross-legged on a tiny ledge, near the top of the sheer Palisades.

At my first *sesshin*, in the hills of Connecticut, he woke up sixty students in the middle of the night and trotted us through the woods into a meadow. The whole universe was on view, as Soen stood in the middle of the field.

— Look up! he cried.

— Swallow the stars to the bottom of your belly!

On the last morning of that retreat, Soen had to give final interviews to all sixty students. If it had been Eido or some other plodding Zen talker, it would have taken all day. But Soen came up with an inspiration.

His *dokusan* room was on the third floor, so each student had to climb two flights of stairs to reach him. As I neared the front of the line, I saw they were coming back down after just a few seconds, many of them weeping. What was he doing?

It turned out he was intercepting us on the second-floor landing, where a window looked out on the rising sun, streaming through the branches of a pine tree. He grabbed each of us as we reached the landing and spun us to face the window. When the sunlight hit me — perfectly centered at the top of this stately tree — I gasped and staggered back. It went right through me. I fell down on the floor and started to worship him. He told me to get up, and rang his bell for the next victim.

Soen's trick was to create a present moment so real that you had to experience it before having any chance to think. It was, literally, "sudden enlightenment."

I WAS LUCKY TO SEE SOEN ROSHI on some of his last trips to America.

He stopped coming after the mid-seventies, as his dream of conquering the West for the *dharma* began to fall apart. The problem was he tried to do it from a distance, with Eido as his emissary and chosen heir. But Eido had a mind of his own.

Once at the Zendo, Eido gave a talk about the flaw in Zen. (In Japanese aesthetics, some flaw is necessary, like the scar in a piece of Raku pottery.) While Zen practice aims at eradicating egoistic thinking, at the same time, he said, it can create a more subtle egoism.

Eido turned out to be the expert on that. Although he bowed to all the idols in the Zendo, and made touching displays of humility before his students, he privately felt that because of his life of spiritual service, he was entitled to anything he wanted.

His style was forceful, bordering on violent. With a stake from wealthy donors, he set out to build the International Dai Bosatsu Monastery in the Catskills, envisioned as a worldwide center for enlightenment. He dictated the design of this grandiose place himself, coming up with something that looked like an airplane hangar on a mountainside. To complete his fantasy, he insisted on raising the water level of Beecher Lake, killing hundreds of trees on the shoreline. To improve the view from the meditation hall, he made students rake the brush and pine-needles from the hillside by the lake, wrecking the ecology of the forest floor and clearing the way for erosion. Finally he wanted to kill off the beavers on the lake, because they disturbed the tranquility of the place with their noisy tail-slapping and unsightly lodge. He was talked out of this by Peter Matthiessen, the writer and naturalist, who warned him it would be bad karma for the monastery.

Peter and I shared a room during a work-week while the monastery was going up. He was one of the Zendo's most important backers, but he seemed gloomy about the whole project. Toward the end of that week the students and volunteers got together for the worst party I ever went to. We passed around a bottle of wine, then sat in silence staring at the fireplace. After a few minutes it became clear this silence was so rigid and tense that nothing could break it. After a half-hour people started drifting off, to a night of bad dreams.

Something was wrong, and it wasn't just the building design. A scandal was brewing, and it soon erupted in a series of angry accusations from women in the group.

Eido's sense of entitlement, it seemed, included all the females in the Zendo. One after another, they came out with stories of him abusing his power, even using the *dokusan* interview to seduce or proposition them. I hadn't suspected — naively — because up to then the women kept it a secret, and Eido was a married man. It turned out Soen had arranged the marriage to try to cool the situation, but it hadn't changed Eido's behavior. Finally the women began to talk to each other, and to protest, and the curtain around the fortress came down.

All this was taking place at the time of the Watergate scandal in Washington, and Eido responded much as Richard Nixon did to the escalating charges against him — with bluster, threats, and non-denial denials.

"Some of these stories are not true," he told a captive audience at the Zendo one night.

"What about the ones that *are* true?" someone shot back.

Eido was appalled that a student would speak out of turn.

But this was America.

"All right," he said. "I will shut up."

LIKE NIXON, THOUGH, Eido didn't get it, and was unable to apologize or change his ways. His followers drifted away, led by a parade of scorned and disillusioned women.

In July 1976 Soen and Eido presided at what was supposed to be a triumphal "Bicentennial *Sesshin*" at the new International Dai Bosatsu Zendo. They had planned for a full house of seekers and dignitaries from all over the world, but only about fifty people showed up, and only about five of them were women.

Midway through one sitting, the fire alarm went off and Eido panicked. He leaped up from his cushion, hyperventilating, and ran out of the room. Was the whole monstrous egotrip now going up in flames? Five minutes later he came back, shaking and gasping with relief, saying it was a false alarm, everything was all right. But it wasn't.

Soen fought for years to bring Eido into line, but he resisted, and it turned into an ugly power struggle between the master and his successor. Soen had given him a *dharma* name that meant "true man with no rank," the very opposite of Eido's authoritarian streak. But it didn't take. Finally the old man gave up and retreated to his mountain fastness in Japan, where he died a few years later.

BY THIS TIME I TOO had drifted away, turned off by the shallowness of Eido's enlightenment, wondering at the flaw in Zen. For several years I sat with a small group of former Zendo members at a loft on 20th Street. We called it the Chelsea Zendo. There we placed our cushions on rough sisal rugs instead of tatami mats, and made do without a teacher.

I wrote to Soen in Japan, but he never answered. Still, I took his *dharma* with me. And it was one of his *haiku* poems that inspired me to go to India.

He wrote in India, "The soul becomes sunburned."

This seemed to contradict two basic tenets of Zen — that there is no soul, and enlightenment is sudden rather than gradual. This made me think some deeper version of truth might be found in that subtle and fragrant land.

11

MOTHER GANGA

I T WAS IN INDIA THAT I LEARNED my next bit of absolute truth, and I did it the time-honored way — traveling around to various ashrams and holy places, failing to find what I was looking for, and then discovering it by accident on my own.

My traveling companion was Arnold "Rusty" Glicksman, a bachelor whose main goal was to get out of America, where he felt depressed. Rusty had grown up in New Jersey but lived in Montreal, where he taught English at a small technical college. He traveled as often as he could, as far away as he could get. He'd been to India before, and loved it for its languor and intensity, its spicy food and beautiful women.

At thirty-six, I was taking a midlife sabbatical — a journey to reflect on the first half of my life, and seek some wisdom that might help me through the rest. I wrote to my kids that whatever happened, they would always come first for me. I felt a little shaky about that. It might reassure them, or at least soften the shock of my leaving the country. But could I keep the promise? All I knew was I could never forget them. I had a premonition I would marry again, and not too far in the future.

OUR FIRST STOP WAS LONDON, where we picked up cheap tickets to Bombay on Air India, and I paid my spontaneous visit to Guy and Luly Wigley. It was my first time in England since I was seven. The hills were just as low and green, and the people just as polite and distant. This was not my destination.

After a few days we flew on to Bombay, and immediately jumped in a taxi for Poona, and the famous ashram of Bhagwan Shree Rajneesh. On the plane, Rusty managed to meet two of Rajneesh's followers, an English couple easily spotted by their orange clothes, and amulets with tiny portraits of the bearded guru. Rusty was as curious as I was about Rajneesh's low road to liberation, which was just then becoming an international scandal. *Time* magazine called him India's "sex guru." His methods seemed to offer a breakthrough from neurotic misery through passionate experience, with fistfights and open sex in the ashram. Still, from his writings, I thought his aims were spiritual.

We introduced ourselves enthusiastically to the English couple, thinking we'd found some kindred spirits. But while they were willing to share a taxi to Poona, they seemed completely uninterested in us. Rusty would ask questions and they would answer as briefly as possible, with a faint air of contempt.

What are your names?

The guy, long-haired and handsome, in his mid-twenties: "My name is Manon."

The woman, slim and voluptuous, a few years older: "My name is Chetan."

Manon and Chetan were also uninterested in the scenery

or the people by the road, and spent most of the hour-long ride kissing, moaning and sighing with the pleasure of it. They were jammed next to me in a small back seat, and I was able to share in the spiritual experience through the pressure of Chetan's undulating rear end against my hip pointer.

Meanwhile I was staring out the window, first at the vast shanty-towns on the outskirts of Bombay, then at the hot and dusty landscape, with people everywhere moving like ants. It was my first day in a poor country, and I found the people's expressions incomprehensible. They seemed grim and single-minded, determined to make their way through another day in an inhospitable world.

In Poona we found a lodge, and made our way on foot to the ashram. The road to liberation was lined with beggars, many with leprosy and missing limbs. I felt foolish heading for a rich man's retreat. Looking for a friend in this new world, I petted a passing goat. He slammed me aside with a head-butt.

At the ashram, a walled compound of pavilions and lush, well-tended gardens, the scene was more familiar but hardly more comforting. Hundreds of Bhagwan's disciples were wandering the grounds, or standing in clumps across the road, littering the dusty shoulder with innumerable cigarette butts. They were all white, mostly European, and all desperate.

Inside the compound, on the main path, we watched a confrontation between two of them. A bearded young man was facing off with a woman, staring fiercely into her eyes from a distance of less than six inches. He hovered over her as if trying to blast something into her brain. She was screaming at him: "You don't know anything about me!" He stared harder, stood his ground. The first to break eye contact would lose the game. She screamed louder: "You fucking asshole!"

Bhagwan Shree Rajneesh had not made these people miserable. They had come here that way, and he was trying to help them in his way. Visitors were welcome and didn't have to pay, but weren't allowed into the intensive workshops where the fighting and open sex took place. We got a good taste of the place, though.

At five a.m. they held a dawn meditation that was the opposite of Zen stillness. For fifty minutes we jumped up and down, vibrating and panting out of rhythm with the live drum music. They called it "chaotic breathing." The instructor told us not to follow any regular rhythm, to deliberately break up any patterns our breath or movements fell into. That's what the mind does, he said, it tries to regularize and impose patterns on experience. We were to break through. And I did.

After fifty minutes the sun had risen and I had a feeling I never had before — exhaustion, an emptiness of mind, an absence of opinions that let me spend the rest of the day in splendid humor, noticing all the bizarre things that went on in the ashram, participating in its curious activities, laughing and letting it be.

My most ecstatic time was in the whirling class, where we learned the basic technique of the Sufi dervishes. Contrary to all my previous learning and experience, I found if you keep one foot in the same place and your eyes on a level plane, it's possible to spin around indefinitely. We beginners did it with one foot planted and the other pushing around in a circle, as if we were riding a scooter on a dime. We held one arm straight and looked out over the fingertips. I felt no dizziness at all. The world, trees, buildings, clouds and sky, just rolled around over and over again like the walls of a whirlpool. The picture was not blurred at all, just moved faster and faster, round and round.

This experience was so deep and inexplicable that I never tried it again after we left the ashram, and to this day don't know if I could repeat it. It seemed like a magical window, opening on an area of truth that could not be set down in words, or summarized on a thumbnail. To say "my true nature is the present moment" is all very well when you're sitting on a cushion staring out into the snowy woods. But when the world is rushing past in an unstoppable continuum, you experience the truth in a different way, speeded up rather than arrested in time. You have no chance to give anything a name. You can't point to a present moment, because it's already past. All that's left is motion and perception, movement and mind, mind moving.

Later it reminded me of a Zen riddle: When the wind blows through the trees, which moves, the wind or the trees?

Answer: The mind moves.

RUSTY AND I STAYED IN POONA only a few days, but we did get to see Rajneesh in action. Once a week he gave a talk, under what news writers call "tight security." To get into the hall you had to walk between two young western women in saris, who sniffed both sides of your head. Apparently the guru was allergic to some common cosmetics, and would go into sneezing fits if certain scents were in the air.

We sat on the floor in the glass-enclosed hall, and Rajneesh spoke for about an hour from a chair on a raised platform. His talk was in Hindi, so we didn't understand a word of it. But we did perceive that he was large and swarthy, and dressed all in white. His tone of voice was alternately boastful, and whining. When he finished speaking he slipped immediately out a side door. Dozens of his devotees came to the edge of the stage, to bow and worship the chair he'd been sitting in. I felt a little foolish, but couldn't resist doing it too. This alarmed Rusty, who thought I'd been converted. I explained that I was just hungry for spiritual kicks, and would try anything.

Both of us concluded that Rajneesh was some kind of legitimate spiritual teacher, but his followers were creeps. However, this didn't seem to make much sense, as the teachings of the guru appeared to exacerbate the worst qualities of his disciples, namely selfishness and viciousness to others.

Once I saw a couple of them, in their saffron robes, screaming at beggar children in the street, threatening them with fists and calling them "filthy little bastards." A few minutes later I was sitting near this couple in a bus, and the woman was beaming with satisfaction. "It feels so good to get my anger out this way," she explained.

All over India, it seemed, the Rajneeshis were notorious for showing no interest in anyone outside their own cult, and treating the Indian people as though they were supposed to be servants at a country club. Whether the guru actually taught this kind of contempt or just failed to address it, we never found out. During our visit to the ashram none of his disciples ever spoke to us, except to answer questions as briefly as possible, and always with that faint air of irritation.

FROM POONA, WE TOOK A TRAIN across India and down the east coast to Madras, the biggest city in south India, and the center of an older, less cosmopolitan civilization, with fewer western tourists. It was in Madras that I felt the first signs of my soul becoming sunburned. We learned how to wear the world's simplest apparel, a *lungi*, an ankle-length skirt folded from a bolt

of cotton cloth. And we learned to eat blazing vegetarian cur-
ries, so hot you felt your head was erupting in flames. The best
meal of my life was a circle of spicy vegetables around a heap
of rice, served on a banana leaf in a tiny cafe by the Indian
Ocean. It cost twenty-five cents.

Life in Madras had many pleasures, but after several weeks
together Rusty and I were getting on each other's nerves, so we
split up. He headed north to Calcutta, and I resumed my spiritual quest, south to Pondicherry, to the ashram and utopian
community founded by the great mystic and philosopher, Sri
Aurobindo.

I expected more of a communal atmosphere at this place
than at Rajneesh's, but it turned out to be just as off-putting
in its way. The residents — mostly elderly, Western, and well-
off — walked around like zombies, lost in thought. The dining
hall served the blandest food in all India, tasteless *chapatis* and
lentil slime with no spices. The sign on the wall read *Silence*,
like the mess hall at Alcatraz. Instead of conversing you were
supposed to meditate on the thought of the day, some profun-
dity about the "higher self" posted at the entrance.

The problem in Pondicherry was that the guru had been
dead for twenty years. Aurobindo's marble tomb, decked with
flowers, was the centerpiece of the ashram. One night they
held a mass meditation around it, and while everyone was very
solemn and still, I noticed that many of the disciples were
falling asleep.

I spent several days hanging around, hoping to break
through the moribund silence, but no one would talk or even
look at me. Finally I thought up a gimmick, and pretended to
be an American reporter writing a piece about their utopia.
After a few rejections I found a young German guy who was

willing to answer questions, though he wouldn't look at me either. He stared off into the treetops and mumbled abstractions, meanwhile shooing beggars with the same contempt if not the same viciousness as Rajneesh's pals.

Once again this was not my destination, so I moved on.

BUDDHISM WAS BORN IN INDIA, but it's no longer practiced there, and most ordinary Indians have never heard of it. Nonetheless I went searching for the roots of Buddhism, and wound up walking around in circles. That's what Buddhist pilgrims do in India. It's called circumambulation, which means walking around a holy place.

In Sarnath, where the Buddha attained his enlightenment, I walked around a great *stupa* — a huge, crumbling pile of bricks built many years ago to commemorate the event. It's set on a neat lawn in a park that reminded me of a military cemetery. Nearby is what's supposed to be an offshoot of the Bo tree under which the Buddha meditated, a perfectly ordinary tree. I had a nice walk, but did not meet the Buddha.

Looking for a live one, I made my way to Dharamsala in the foothills of the Himalayas, and walked around the compound of the Dalai Lama, the exiled god-king of Tibetan Buddhism. His house was on a hilltop and protected by a high fence, but you could circumambulate through the woods outside.

On my way I passed a young Buddhist nun who was circumambulating the place on her face. Rather than walking she was diving into one prostration after another, crawling along the half-mile path. She was panting with fatigue and misery, her face and clothes all smeared with mud.

Hundreds of monks and nuns lived what appeared to be an aimless existence in Dharamsala. They seemed to have no knowledge or interests outside of Buddhism, which they had reduced to mechanical practices and games, such as spinning prayer wheels in the marketplace. Spinning the wheel saves you the trouble of saying a prayer. Many of the monks were in excellent shape from doing hundreds of prostrations every morning and evening. I watched one who had outfitted himself with a pair of lambs-wool sliding pads, so he could hit the floor with the heels of his hands and slide out flat without a hitch. The stone floor beneath him was polished smooth.

For entertainment, the monks would sit in tea-houses, drink hot water with lemon and engage in chanting duels. They would face off across a table and go for the deepest, most guttural and sepulchral roar, then laugh and have some more hot water.

Possibly in Tibet itself, isolated on the roof of the world, the life of ritual still had some spiritual value. But in Dharamsala, where the tea-houses were full of rug dealers, drug dealers and Western TV crews, it seemed meaningless.

THE RIVER GANGES BEGINS with mountain springs and melting snow in the Himalayas, and flows down onto the great fertile plain of northern India, 1,560 miles to Calcutta and the Indian Ocean. That's the physical description, but in India there is always a parallel spiritual account of things, and in this "Mother Ganga" descends from heaven and flows through various holy sites, and the holiest of these is Benares.

At the holy city of Hardwar, where the river sluices down from the Himalayan foothills, it's a cold, rushing stream. Pilgrims hang onto metal frames by the riverbank to keep from being swept downstream.

Five hundred miles east in Benares, it's deep and full, warm and placid, like a cow. Bathing in the Ganges at Hardwar is like having your sins washed away; bathing at Benares is like being forgiven.

You don't need a guru in Benares. All you need is to sit on the *ghats* by the river, by the shrines and temples and the open-air crematorium, and watch the hubbub of life and death meet the peace of the river. The longer you sit, the better it gets.

Near the top of the stairs where the main road spills down toward the riverbank, you pass a tiny temple tucked in between buildings. It's a room about twelve feet by ten, open to the street. There every day from dawn to dusk, Hindus hold a service that consists of a chant, sung responsively and repeated endlessly with varying melodies and rhythms. The words are:

> *Si Ram Jay Ram*
> *Jay Jay Ram.*

I couldn't translate it and didn't care to, but I sang it for hours every day. Anyone could come in, sit down on the rug and join in. The leader played a harmonium, a small keyboard instrument like an accordion, and they had a tabla drum and some small cymbals for rhythm. After a while I picked up the cymbals and became a regular member of the band.

Like all bands, it had its ups and downs. One of the leaders seemed a bit egotistical, hurried the tempo and didn't seem to be listening. But then there was an older woman who gave the chant a slow, mysterious reading, almost like a romantic song. Another man wailed it like a lament, but with joy and passion in it. Or maybe that was just the way I sang it to myself.

One day, in the middle of a bright, sunny afternoon, I was playing the cymbals and looking out over the river. The

Ganges seemed completely smooth, with all its motion under the surface. From shore to shore, you could see the curvature of the earth. On the near bank, workmen were digging ground for a new temple. Cows wandered around the broad stairs amid the pilgrims and tourists.

Si Ram Jay Ram seemed effortless, just spinning itself out over and over again. Suddenly it struck me I had become part of this group of Hindus, part of the music itself. How could this be? I knew nothing about them, not even their names. I didn't belong to their religion or understand their language. A thought occurred, almost casually: *I guess we're all just brothers and sisters.*

A few seconds later, I realized I had just uttered the most hackneyed of all absolute truths. But I had come to it innocently, with a beginner's mind. It was the only way to explain my own happiness.

Thinking about it later, it did not escape me that this insight was not just a universal truth, but a particularly Christian thought. It was the last kind of revelation I expected in India.

Before my travels I'd been carrying on a running feud about Christianity with my friend Debra Given. She was a divinity student at Yale, a former teenage "Jesus freak" and still a bit narrow-minded in my view, at least on the topic of personal salvation. She was also warm and sunny, and unusually innocent for a 23-year-old. We met the year before she went to Yale, when she was living on 18th Street, two blocks from me, and working as a clerk-typist. We both went to country dances in the Village.

Debra gave me her version of Christianity, that it was her path to truth, goodness and meaning in life. I gave her mine, that it was a backward and primitive faith. My chief complaint was its dualism — the separation of God from humans, heaven from earth, the body from the spirit, Christians from heathens. There seemed no room in this system for my prized enlightenment, where the relative and the absolute become one. Or was that what Jesus Christ was supposed to represent? Even so, that was just a folk tale. In a sophisticated religion you don't need a legendary character to solve the riddle. You can do it yourself, right?

In this manner I berated Debra on long walks by the Hudson River, around the Croton Reservoir near her parents' home in Peekskill, over *arroz con pollo* in a Cuban-Chinese diner on Eighth Avenue. By my scorecard I won at least fourteen out of fifteen rounds in this intellectual bout. That didn't bother her, because she wasn't keeping score. She said she enjoyed arguing with me, and her faith seemed impervious to attack. She was going to be a Presbyterian minister.

I WASN'T AWARE THAT CHRISTIANITY existed in India, except for missionary work, but there I learned it's been around since the early days of the church. In Madras I was taken to see the Church of St. Thomas, supposedly founded by the doubting apostle in the Gospel of John. I doubted it. But I did see that Christians were an influential minority in India, and stood out in contrast to the Hindus, Muslims and Sikhs.

I had always thought of Christians as prudes, but in India they were the most liberal group. The only Indian women who would talk to us were Christians. Rusty and I fell in with a group of young single women on the train to Madras, and we chatted away for hours. They thought we were Christians too, and were amazed to learn that one was a Buddhist and the other a Jew. The most talkative of the group, a slim, pretty girl who wore an Indian-style pants suit instead of a sari, told us several times that she and her companions were "all from different castes," but still traveling together. That was meaningless to us, but apparently a bold gesture of liberation in India.

By the time we got to Madras, Rusty claimed he was "in love" with the pants-suited one. But the girls went off with their chaperone and we were too shy to chase them.

THE BROAD OCEAN BEACH at Madras serves as an open-air market and culture festival, and we would walk there at sunset to watch everything from drilling army reservists to snake-charmers with cobras. One evening a young man rushed up and pleaded for help. He said he had to write a letter in English, some kind of appeal for a local charity. It turned out he was a Christian, and his cause was the Sisters of Charity, the order founded by Mother Teresa of Calcutta. In return for my editorial assistance, he took me on tour of their local operations, an orphanage and a home for retarded children.

These places were like nothing else I saw in India. At the orphanage, the children were the same as the little ones dying on the sidewalks, with flies buzzing around their eyes. But here they were clean and eating rice in a quiet circle, with a Sister dressed in blue. The saying posted on the wall was from Jesus, about "the least of these."

At the home for retarded children, they lay in deformed heaps on mats, but in their eyes, and the Sisters' eyes, was serenity, even happiness.

I felt unworthy of these sights. Of course, the tour was a fund-raising appeal — every Westerner in India was seen as a potential donor. So I gave them a few of my rupees, and ran. My guide offered to take to me to a hospice for the dying homeless, but I couldn't take any more.

In Calcutta a few weeks later, a fellow traveler told me she had seen a man die on the street, and she'd run to tell a policeman.

— Don't worry about it, said the cop. It's only a beggar.

From Delhi I wrote to Debra to apologize for my ignorant attacks on the religion of compassion and grace.

When I got back, I called her up. She said thanks for the letter. She was going out with a fellow seminarian who was interested in Zen Buddhism, she said.

WHO'S WHO: DEBRA GIVEN, PRESBYTERIAN MINISTER.

Height: five foot two

Eyes: blue

Hair: blonde, wavy

Outstanding physical characteristics: broad, frequent, radiant smile. Clear, sweet voice, whether speaking or singing.

Purpose in life: "to do the Lord's work."

Married 7/7/79 to Thomas Phillips.

12

THE STUMBLING BLOCK

D EBRA AND I WERE MARRIED a little more than a year after I got
back from India. It was a surprise to both of us. She had
gone off to divinity school with the idea of meeting a nice Christian man, and combining marriage with ministry. Somehow, it
didn't work out. I like to think it was because her boyfriends
paled in comparison to me, but according to her, she was just
too shy to talk to the men who really attracted her at Yale.

During this time I held little hope, but kept myself around
just in case. I became friends with her older sister Linda, also
a country dancer, and her younger sister Nancy, who was living
in the Village and studying art at Cooper Union. Debra liked
that family connection so much that she tried to set up a match
between Linda and me. I would have none of it. I wouldn't
squander what little chance I had by getting involved with her
sister.

Still, I took Debra at her word that she wouldn't marry a
non-Christian. I wished her happiness, but made it clear I
loved her and, if she ever changed her mind, would be willing

to sacrifice my solitude for her. I liked living alone and meditating in peace, and wouldn't have given it up for anyone else. But I knew the rest of my life would feel like a country-music tragedy if I just stood back and let her marry someone else.

A new opportunity came up in the fall of 1978, when she returned to New York for a year's internship at Convent Avenue Baptist Church in Harlem. Just back from India, I got a part-time position teaching journalism at City College, which happened to be a few blocks from the church. Once or twice a week we met by a falafel stand at the college to eat lunch and chat.

She also invited me to her dorm room at Union Theological Seminary to play tunes on her guitar and my fiddle. This was all very pleasant, but I had learned not to get my hopes up. Still I got an odd sensation one day when she complained of a pain in her hand, and I showed her a massage technique I'd learned from the Tibetans, pushing my thumb gently into the hollows between the bones.

— That feels good, she said, several times.

A few weeks later she invited me to Thanksgiving dinner with her family in Peekskill, and that odd sensation returned when, after dinner, she sat down next to me on the couch. Instead of the usual reserve, I was picking up a feeling of openness and warmth, a long-looked-for invitation.

I just sat there.

Maybe it was wariness after being rejected for so long. Or maybe it was fear of screwing it up, and turning my country-music tragedy into a true disaster. In any case, I let the invitation lie there for weeks.

Finally, the sisters switched roles. Linda called me to say Debra was upset that I was paying no attention to her. So I called her.

We met at my house for a negotiating session.

— OK, I said, I'll be your boyfriend, but only if you're serious about this, even to the point of marriage.

— I'm open to it, she said.

After that we exchanged a few tentative hugs and kisses, and I walked her to the subway. Going through the turnstile she put on a show of mock romance, clutching her hands over her heart like Juliet. I waved and shook my head ruefully.

I turned away with one thought: This is not going to work.

MY MOTHER TOLD ME THE KEY to a happy marriage is "the same brand of humor," something she didn't have with my father. I'd used this criterion in choosing my first wife, who laughed at my jokes. But Debra didn't meet the test at all. My literary references were lost on her, while her brand of humor was sight-gags and funny faces. She was also eleven years younger and nearly a foot shorter. What did we have to go on?

Plato knew. In the *Symposium* he has Socrates prove that love is not finding someone just like you. It is searching for something you lack, in someone you crave because they have what you don't. Debra had faith, and the willingness to put it to work. I wanted to be part of that work, even if I didn't have faith. And maybe, in time, I would learn how she did it.

I got a clue that Easter. Debra invited me and my children to the seminary to decorate Easter eggs, with her sister Nancy. I was nervous, because the kids barely knew her. But every trace of discomfort dissolved as soon as we set to work dyeing and painting the dozens of eggs she had ready. This was pure fun for her, but she also knew how to include others in her fun, even putting their enjoyment before hers. She made sure everyone had something to do, and no one felt their product was inferior.

I knew I couldn't marry anyone unless my children were comfortable with her. I'd had another girlfriend the year before who was good enough with kids, but guarded with her own feelings. She had a certain amount of love to give out, and didn't want to squander it unless she was sure of getting something in return.

Debra was indiscriminate in loving. It pleased her, and she didn't worry about squandering it, because it flowed from her like an inexhaustible spring.

We spent the afternoon in pure pleasure, with none of the usual resentments among Jenny, Luke, and Django. A middle child herself, Debra understood how Luke could get lost in the shuffle, and Django could feel dumb just because he was the youngest. Everyone seemed to understand we were in good hands, and could relax.

Afterwards, she walked us to the subway. Django meandered up Broadway, looking up at the sky like a drunk. "Thank you," he kept saying, "Thank you for everything."

FOR MY FIRST WEDDING I had rented a tuxedo. For this one, at Yorktown Presbyterian Church, I wore my own clothes — a white Indian shirt, white painter's pants, and flip-flops. Debra wore a white blouse and a purple-printed Indian skirt, with flowers in her hair.

For the cover of the church program, we wrote out a verse from a Bob Dylan song:

> O sister, am I not a brother to you,
> And one deserving of affection?
> And is our purpose not the same on this earth,

To love and follow his direction?

Luke, thirteen, was the best man. Jenny, fifteen, was the bridesmaid, and nine-year-old Django the ring bearer. A hundred or so people attended, including country dancers, divinity students, Zen students, church members and clergy from Harlem, and writers from CBS.

We wrote our own vows, and exchanged them under the pastoral blessing of Debra's divinity school roommate, the Rev. Emma Jane Finney. We promised each other "to be with you and guard your solitude, so that each of us alone and both of us together may become all we are called to be, for ourselves and others."

Jennifer said she stood there shaking through the whole ceremony. I shook too, but it was a pleasurable sensation, the height of intensity and intention. After church we repaired to a nearby farm for a buffet lunch and country dancing on the lawn. The climax of the feast was a carrot cake.

Around sunset we drove off to the Catskills for a few days' honeymoon in a friend's cabin. The first night was fine — we were exhausted, but inspired by the day's celebration. The next day I drove us to a nearby meditation center to see Swami Muktananda from India. I had fun, chanting in Sanskrit and prostrating myself before the guru, who rewarded me with a swat from his peacock-feather fan. But Debra, the whitewashed Presbyterian, was turned off by the Hindu hubbub. For starters, she said the décor looked like a six-year-old's birthday party.

We had our first marital squabble that night, lasting for hours and ending with a discussion of the divinity of Jesus, which I didn't believe in. That was round one of a wrestling match that lasted nearly ten years.

For our first Christmas together, I gave Debra a Zen meditation cushion, and she gave me an *Oxford Annotated Bible*. The deal was that I would try her spiritual practice if she would try mine.

IF IT'S POSSIBLE TO MAKE a slow-motion leap of faith, in tiny steps over many years, that's roughly what I did. I immersed myself in Christianity a bit at a time, assuring myself it was just an experiment and I could withdraw at will.

I began by editing Debra's sermons, reading the Bible passages and using my English-major skills to pull meaning out of the text. All I needed was a "suspension of disbelief" to become caught up in the gospels, in Jesus' ministry, his passion, death and resurrection. Still, I told myself, this was just literary work.

Then Debra recruited me to teach Sunday School at her church. My job was to get a class of half-asleep teenagers excited about the Bible, and I succeeded some of the time by asking provocative questions.

One Sunday I gave them a multiple-choice about Jesus Christ. What is he, a friend, teacher, or savior? Most of the kids said teacher, but one thirteen-year-old girl wasn't happy with that. Suddenly sitting up, she argued that he had more than a message, he was something in himself. A savior? Well, yes.

I felt thrilled with the lesson, even though I couldn't personally accept the conclusion. Ordinary people might need a savior, but not someone like me.

As the years went on though, a feeling of envy grew for those who did have a savior. At Easter the choir would sing the "Hallelujah Chorus" from *The Messiah*, and I could barely keep my voice steady while intoning the prophetic words.

I allowed myself to experience the feeling, like peering into the gates of Heaven. But when it was over and the organ thunder died down, I went back to my little cave of secular wisdom. I couldn't really believe, "The kingdom of this world has become the kingdom of our Lord and of his Christ." Could I?

Still I envied the folk who walked out of church glowing on Easter Sunday. So after years of feeling deprived, I decided to join the church, and become an official Christian at least on the outside. I figured this would be easy enough — many members didn't really believe in the church's radical views, and I could slip in among them, partaking in the comforts of faith at little cost. Better a bad Christian than a man without a spiritual home.

Debra didn't raise any objection to this, but to my surprise I hit resistance at a higher level. By this time she was associate minister at Broadway Presbyterian Church in Manhattan, so I took my application to the chief pastor, the Rev. Carl Rosenblum. I told him I wanted to join because I liked the people and the atmosphere at church, enjoyed his sermons as well as my wife's, and liked singing in the choir.

To my amazement, he put a stumbling block in my path, in the form of a prescribed question which he treated as a real question: "Do you accept Jesus Christ as your Lord and Savior?"

— Well, I don't know about that, I said.

— Well, then, he said gently, come back when you do.

I walked out shocked at his behavior. I'd always assumed Christians were hypocrites, and would be just as happy with simulated faith as real faith. But this was no hypocrite. Rosenblum came from a poor, unhappy family, and had been converted as a desperate teenager by a Methodist evangelist. Faith was all that stood between him and despair, and he expected it to be just as important to his parishioners. Could I identify with this?

I contemplated it walking the streets for the next few days and nights. The next Sunday, Rosenblum used me as an anonymous example in his sermon, a case of a man searching for faith. He concluded:

— And where is that man today? I don't know.

My problem was that faith could not be soaked up casually, like the atmosphere at the church coffee hour. It needed an active step across the threshold, a risk I didn't know if I was willing to take. Once again, I had to become "desperated."

In fact I wasn't far from despair. My desire to join the church was deeper than it appeared; otherwise, I would have given up at the first sign of resistance. It was the same desire that took me to the Zendo, to India, and down the aisle with Debra. I wanted to be saved, and not just in the abstract. I needed to be saved, from chronic feelings of failure and defeat, inadequacy and guilt, feelings that seemed to run deeper than anything I could muster against them.

I went back to talk to Rosenblum, several times. I had to admit I could use a savior, I just didn't know if this was the one.

One gray morning in November, I took the subway at rush hour, and stepped onto the long escalator at the Columbus Circle station. I looked up and saw an endless procession of workers, silent and slumped, riding from the gloom of the subway to the gloom of the street. On the down escalator, another endless line was making the journey in reverse.

I was almost ready to cry. Instead I prayed, putting everything I had into the shortest prayers I knew:

— Lord, have mercy, I said. Nothing happened.

— Christ, have mercy, I said. And something happened.

It felt like a giant can-opener came down and slit my back, laying me open to a cataract of water that poured down and bathed my soul. I shook my head and shuddered in my shoes. The escalator dumped me at the street level and I wandered out into the winter light. The water was still flowing, in an endless stream.

What is this?

As Soen Roshi said when I solved his Zen riddle, "No need give it a name."

A few Sundays later, I was baptized by the Rev. Rosenblum at Broadway Presbyterian Church, after answering the standard question.

"Who is your Lord and Savior?"

"Jesus Christ is my Lord and Savior."

Debra stood by and wept, and embraced me when it was over.

Someone asked me how I felt. Embarrassed, I said. I had lost my contest with Debra, and opened myself to the world's ridicule. My only consolation was the promise of mercy, in an endless stream.

13

THE GROVES OF ACADEME

D EBRA AND I WERE BOTH UNEMPLOYED when we got married, but within a year she had her first call, assistant minister at the Presbyterian Church in Mount Vernon, New York; and I had my first full-time teaching job, assistant professor at the Columbia School of Journalism.

For years I had wanted to teach journalism — to be in touch with the world and help people write about it, but without the corporate pressures of CBS. Columbia seemed the perfect opportunity — bright students, in the atmosphere of a great university.

At the School of Journalism I taught radio and TV news, exactly as I would if I'd become the producer of the nightly news at Channel Eleven. There was no coddling in my newsroom — we actually tried to cover the news of the day in New York. I advertised my workshop as a "zoo," and taught by yelling and screaming, mocking and cheering, blatantly favoring smart students over the plodders, and throwing tantrums when people wouldn't co-operate. It was, as one student said, "the real world." I thought that was appropriate. This was a one-year master's program, and these students were soon to enter the marketplace. However, some of my faculty colleagues were offended, and tried to foil me.

One year I got back from Christmas vacation to find the curriculum for the workshop had been changed. The associate dean called me in and handed me the new lesson plan. Students would no longer be required to complete a piece in one day! Instead they could have two full days to write and edit, and the workshop would be an hour-long magazine-type show once a week, rather than a nightly newscast Thursday and Friday. This was the work of some of my broadcast colleagues, who preferred "thoughtful feature pieces" to breaking news. But this was the spring semester. In a few weeks, these students would be looking for jobs in local TV news. They had to know how to do hard news, on a hard deadline, the same day. Besides, that was what I knew. I was "Tom Tonight." My way of handling this academic in-fight was to accept the piece of paper with the new curriculum, and ignore it. I was still the main teacher in the TV workshop, the only one who had experience putting on a whole newscast, and I would teach it the way I always had. No one stepped up to challenge my academic freedom to do that, so the workshop went on as usual.

As a Columbia professor, I had serious deficiencies. The emphasis at the J-school was newspaper reporting, and everyone had to teach a basic course in it. I didn't know the ropes of newspaper reporting. We also had to supervise master's projects, long-form magazine-type pieces, another area where I had little experience. So I was faking my way through the core curriculum while putting most of my passion into the radio and

TV workshops.

Still, I had some wonderful students, and steered a few into careers in TV news. These were the ones who actually thrived on my teaching methods, who liked to learn by doing, under the gun. Leigh Ann Winick was so cool and reliable that just a few years later I recruited her on short notice to sub for a writer on the *CBS Evening News*. She slipped into that seat with no preparation, and wrote like she'd been doing it for years. She went on to produce for CNN and CBS.

Tom Rosenstiel was calm and thoughtful beyond his years, able to wrap his head around a breaking story as big and unexpected as the failed US rescue mission of the hostages in Iran. It was his turn to anchor the news in the TV workshop that night in 1980, and he made more sense of the story than many of the network news stars. After a few years of newspaper reporting, he founded the Project for Excellence in Journalism, becoming a respected critic of the news media. Later he became executive director of the American Press Institute.

My best student ever was one I expected to be the worst. Glancing at Tom Grant's bio in the 1986 student handbook, I was shocked. He looked like a truck driver, and his credentials didn't look much better — a B.A. from Washington State University, then a series of jobs with small-town newspapers in the Pacific Northwest. What was he doing among the elites at Columbia?

Tom Grant turned out to be the best reporter I ever had at the school — a relentless investigator who knew how to read budgets and court records, and how to talk to people. Tom had trouble with some of the faculty because he never passed up a battle. If he thought you were wrong, he'd say so. When it came to TV, though, he knew nothing, and soaked up every instruction we gave. By the end of the workshop he was able to write and produce, and even talk like a pro on TV in his straightforward, urgent style.

After graduating Tom went to work for a Vermont TV station, and a few years later was back in the Northwest, reporting for the CBS affiliate in Spokane, where he uncovered the biggest story of his life. On a tip, he began investigating a lurid story in the small city of Wenatchee, 165 miles from Spokane. Police there were charging people in connection with an alleged child sex ring, centered in a Pentecostal church. The charges were sensational — including orgies of child sex abuse on the altar of the church. Dozens of people were accused — ten were convicted, eighteen others pleaded guilty.

The whole thing turned out to be a witch hunt — a fantasy built on evidence from a couple of underage false witnesses, fed by a whole town's hysteria. But the local media reported the charges as if they were true. Tom was alone in raising questions, talking to the townspeople and the accused. He kept at it for nine months, filing more than 150 stories for KREM-TV, not putting in for his overtime because he knew management would object and might pull him off the story. In the end the victims of the Wenatchee witch hunt were all exonerated, and freed. Many were the least able to defend themselves – poor, illiterate, or retarded.

Tom became nationally known for the story, and came back to New York to accept the George Polk Award and the DuPont-Columbia Award. At the Polk ceremony, he mumbled something about doing it "for the least of these."

What I loved about Tom Grant was that, like Debra, he had something I lacked — in his case a strict moral code, along with the skills, strength and stamina to make it work for others. He felt an imperative to do that, no matter what the cost.

The Wenatchee story was the peak of his career. Besides the Polk and DuPont awards, it won him a fellowship at the University of Michigan. But when he went back to Spokane, KREM declined to rehire him. He wound up at another station, but within a couple of years quit in disgust, fed up with TV, fed up with bosses who were afraid of controversy. He went back to print journalism, but it was the same story there, even at so-called alternative newspapers.

Still, the story may have a happy ending. After earning a Ph.D. in media ethics at the University of Idaho, today he's a professor, in charge of the journalism program at a little state college in Georgia — Abraham Baldwin Agricultural College. As students go, his are "the least of these," back-country kids who know little of the great world. Among his course offerings are a TV workshop, much like the one at the Columbia J-school. He's also the adviser to the student newspaper, and I've advised him against launching any investigations of the school or the town. Stay in school, I say, get your tenure.

When I landed in a professor's chair at Columbia, I was only dimly aware of the distinction between tenured and non-tenured faculty. I thought they were lucky to get me, as most TV news professionals wouldn't consider a switch to the low-paying field of education. In my arrogant way I acted as if I already had tenure — speaking my mind at faculty meetings, sassing the dean, and exercising my academic freedom to do what I wanted. The first week of class I found they had given me what I thought was an unreasonable schedule, forcing me to spend a night correcting papers from a newspaper course, in between teaching a radio workshop all day, two days in a row. So I told them to get someone else for one of the radio days. I was warned by a senior faculty member that I was becoming a *cause celebre*, but I brushed that off as mere ruffled feathers.

Unfortunately in academia, ruffled feathers tend to stay that way. I got off to a bad start with the dean and the tenured faculty, and never was able to ingratiate myself with the old guard. The dean paid me back with petty assignments, like serving as a marshal on graduation day.

Still, teaching was a sweet deal. The pay wasn't great, but we got a subsidized apartment on 113th Street, generous benefits and plenty of free time. I made up a song, to the tune of a sea chantey, "Rolling Down to Old Maui."

> *It's a damn tough life, full of toil and strife*
> *We professors undergo.*
> *We don't give a damn when the year is o'er*
> *How much the students know.*
> *We're vacation bound, it's a grand old sound,*
> *With the wife and familee,*
> *And we don't give a damn for the world outside*
> *Of the Groves of Academe!*

This is sung with four syllables to "academe," the emphasis on the "me." This little ditty annoyed my wife, who doesn't share my brand of humor and has never sympathized with my lazy or cynical streaks.

In 1986 I made my bid for tenure, and was rejected by the faculty of journalism. Angry and miserable for a while, I was soon grateful to my deliverers. I landed back in the real world, for the biggest stories of my life.

1989

AFTER SEVEN YEARS OF EXILE IN ACADEME, I managed to get back to CBS for a once-in-a-lifetime era of news, coinciding with the tenure of Tom Bettag as executive producer of the *Evening News*. Still in his thirties, Tom was a gentleman with a kid's enthusiasm for the job. His favorite phrase was "Would you dare?" which he used to preface one wild idea after another, all designed to cover the news faster and better than anyone in the world. His favorite stunts were spur-of-the-moment flights to the ends of the earth, in pursuit of stories that sometimes happened and sometimes didn't. That was no problem, though. Tom could take you from anywhere to anywhere quicker than anyone, and if he miscalculated in the morning he could usually fix it by evening, and parachute into the right place in time to fight his way onto the air at 6:30 New York time. He was also able and willing to work twenty-four hours a day, for up to a week.

In these adventures he had an ideal partner in Dan Rather, who was eager to go anywhere under any conditions — the more difficult and dangerous, the better — to beat his more reflective rivals at the other networks.

Bettag hired me as the foreign writer shortly after he took over, as part of a team that turned the anchor desk into an airborne operation, racing around the world to cover a period of revolutionary change. While Tom and Dan fought their way onto the air, it was my job to come up with a script, often ripped out of a notepad in the last few minutes before air. By reading the spots off the papers and skimming a history book or two on the plane, I could make it sound as if we'd been studying the situation calmly and deliberately, when in fact we had just landed in a strange capital at night, and sprinted to a hotel balcony with a camera and a satellite dish.

Three squares stand out in my memory of this period: Red Square in Moscow, Wenceslas Square in Prague, and Tiananmen Square in Beijing.

We went to Moscow at least once a year from 1987 to 1991, as Mikhail Gorbachev tried to rescue the Soviet Union from collapse. My first look at Moscow was a revelation.

Like all Americans, I'd been taught — both by my anti-communist teachers and my communist friends — that the Soviet Union was an economic superpower, and a godless state. A drive from the airport to Red Square, and a day spent contemplating the Kremlin, were enough to convince me that neither was true.

Moscow looked more like India than America. The streets were filthy, the stores empty, the people deprived and depressed. They walked the streets with plastic mesh shopping bags, and would run to join any line they saw, because it meant some scarce item of consumer goods had appeared. They lined up for milk, beer, shoddy clothes, coffee, soap. Imports from outside the Soviet bloc were illegal, and priceless.

At the Hotel Rossiya, we were cautioned to unplug our television sets after turning them off. Soviet TVs were known to explode without warning. I made the mistake of sending some clothes to the hotel laundry; only about half of them came back. Buying a hot dog at the cafeteria, I gave the cashier a ruble, and was puzzled when she gave me only about half the change I was expecting. I inquired, and she yelled at me.

— I don't have any more!

On Red Square, I didn't have enough rubles to buy a watercolor of St. Basil's Cathedral from a sidewalk artist. At the official exchange rate, he wanted about forty dollars. I offered him ten dollars in US currency, and he snapped it up like a lottery prize.

Short of producers on one trip, Bettag sent me with a camera crew to an auto factory on the outskirts of Moscow. It looked like an American plant, but the assembly line was stalled most of the time, while the workers sat around talking and smoking. They couldn't finish the cars because they didn't have all the parts. I interviewed the manager, a swarthy guy who looked like a poster boy for Soviet industry. He was desperate.

— Can you send me an American? he begged. Somebody from Chrysler, to help us?

Still, I was impressed with Russia. I never set foot outside the capital, but you could feel the essence of Russia in the heart of Moscow, in Red Square and the Kremlin. It made Washington, DC, seem like a city without a soul.

I learned from my history book that Moscow was originally a religious capital, the seat of the Russian Orthodox Church. Red Square and the Kremlin take up only about a square mile, at the city's highest elevation, but that mile seems to represent the whole nation.

The square itself, not square but oblong, not flat but rolling like the curve of the Earth, feels like the vast Russian prairie, the steppes. At either end are icons of Russian history, symbols of extremism bordering on insanity: St. Basil's, a multicolored explosion of onion domes built by Ivan the Terrible in the fifteenth century; and Lenin's Tomb, the morbid mausoleum of a fanatic who tried to replace the soul of Mother Russia with heavy machinery.

Looming over it all is the Kremlin, a filigreed fortress that contains, not just cannons, but medieval cathedrals, and a museum of golden crowns, royal carriages, and bejeweled Easter eggs. The long row of evergreens under the Kremlin wall I took as a symbol of the Russian people. Though they were silent and unimposing, nothing could wilt them — not fire or 50-below-zero cold, not Napoleon or Hitler, Lenin or Stalin, nor any of the lunatics plotting the next revolution.

An old Moscow mother cackled as we interviewed her about the people's view of politics.

— We're nothing but subjects in one crazy experiment after another, she said. But we'll always get along.

— How?

— By stealing from the state!

IN THE END, OF COURSE, the Soviet state collapsed of its own hollowness, when there was little left to steal. The implosion started in Europe, on the rim of the Soviet empire in the 1980s, and reached critical mass in 1989.

Two weeks after the fall of the Berlin Wall, we were preparing to fly to Rome for the meeting of Gorbachev and Pope John Paul II, the first-ever meeting between a Soviet leader and a

Pope. Then Bettag got a tip from a high-ranking U.S. diplomat that Czechoslovakia, which was invaded and occupied when it tried to defy the Soviets in 1968, was about to rise up again, and this time the outcome would be different. Bettag grabbed me in the hallway, grinning the grin he couldn't suppress when he knew he was ahead of the competition. "Think Prague," he said. The next day we were stealing into the Czech capital in a snowstorm, just in time for the revolution.

Czechoslovakia had all the marks of a communist state in an advanced state of decay. The airport stank of dirt and cheap tobacco, and the customs police were drunk. Through some mix-up I was last to go through customs, so I had to fill out a declaration for a trunk full of TV equipment. I had no idea what it was, so I just made a list of technical-sounding names like "transformer." The glassy-eyed agent looked at it for a second, then waved me through.

On the road into Prague we saw forlorn people standing at filthy bus shelters, and then an amazing sight — a stadium full of young people, chanting and shouting. For a moment I thought I was back in Iowa, because it looked like a pep rally for a college football game, right down to the clothes and the faces of the students. They were all wearing American-style parkas or down jackets with stocking caps, and the faces were light-skinned, dark-haired and square-jawed, like typical Iowans. CBS News correspondent Richard Threlkeld, a Minnesota native, reminded me that the Czechs of Bohemia had emigrated to the Midwest in the early twentieth century. These students were descendants of the same people, but this rally had nothing to do with football. They were leading the revolution.

The center of Prague that night looked like a winter Woodstock. Thousands of students were holding hands in a great circle around St. Vitus Cathedral at the top of the city's highest hill, winding through the streets in the snow, singing. They weren't afraid of the government any more. "It's just a bunch of tinkers and tailors," one of our guides snorted. She was right. The communists were a pathetic lot, the only ones left willing to follow orders from Moscow. But now, no orders were coming from Moscow, and the tinkers and tailors were on their own.

The government was in disarray, facing the threat of a general strike that amounted to a referendum on communist rule. They appointed several new leaders in a week, ending up with a party hack named Urbanek, who went out onto a factory floor with this hapless advice to the workers:

— Don't strike, he said. You might get in trouble.

The students and intellectuals weren't afraid any more, but the workers were still the key. Would they fall for this?

The strike was called for noon on November 30, with a rally in Wenceslas Square. We set ourselves up in the Hotel Jalta, a stinking dump overlooking the square. Dan and a cameraman were on the balcony in 35-degree cold, Tom was standing in the open window with headphones on to talk to New York, and I was in the unheated hotel room at my manual typewriter, with one eye on the square outside and the other on Czech TV, where we could see what was happening in the rest of the country. We knew the Russians were not going to invade, but we didn't know if the workers would be able to set aside their memories and defy the government. And we didn't know what the police would do.

The answer came at noon. The whistle blew and workers began pouring into the square, stamping and roaring. Within minutes the huge square, ten blocks long, was filled, and the hotel was shaking with the uproar. Czech TV reported it was the same everywhere, not a single worker left on a factory floor. The police just stood by. We interviewed a spokesman for the strikers, and he was laughing.

— I think I'm the new defense minister, he said.

In fact it took a few more days for the tinkers and tailors to understand, and resign. A new government took over, with Vaclav Havel, the playwright and former political prisoner, elected president. This was the "Velvet Revolution," won without a shot fired or a blow struck. Czechoslovakia shook off forty years of communist rule and returned almost immediately to Western civilization. When we went back two years later, the airport was clean and modern; the Hotel Jalta had a gleaming interior and didn't stink. And everywhere, you saw billboards with the Marlboro Man, by then an outcast in America, riding a new range in central Europe.

The Velvet Revolution was inspiring, but seemed a bit unreal. It was tempting to think it succeeded because the corrupt powers were overwhelmed by the idealism and courage of the people. It probably looked that way in our CBS News coverage. But the truth was it succeeded because Czechoslovakia was a cold-war puppet state, and behind the scenes the puppeteer had pulled out.

THINGS WERE DIFFERENT IN CHINA, where a much bigger uprising came to grief.

Before and after the massacre in Tiananmen Square, the Chinese government put out the story that this was a counter-revolutionary uprising orchestrated by a small group. Party leader Deng Hsiao-Ping may have believed that, but he wasn't there, and no one who was there believes it. No one has ever seen protests on the scale that swept China in 1989.

Tienanmen is ten times the size of Wenceslas Square, a huge stretch of concrete in the middle of Beijing with a giant portrait of Mao Zedong at one end. At the height of the uprising about a million people were occupying the square. Students were the leaders, but everyone else was represented, too. They came in groups identified with banners — nurses, artists, hotel workers. I knew it was a general uprising when a truck swept in filled with workers shouting and waving brooms. It was the garbage collectors.

The student leaders, demanding democracy, set up their own little democracy in the square. Everything had to be voted on. We saw it in action when producer Susan Zirinsky and I, rushing back to the hotel, took a shortcut across the square. On the perimeter a fence was in our way, right next to a student command post. Zirinsky, the legendary hard-driving producer, was not about to turn back. She pleaded with the students, dropping the names of their leaders, saying all we were trying to do was get their story out. They huddled and voted, all their hands shooting up simultaneously. We won, and jumped the fence.

The students loved our presence, and welcomed us every morning as we arrived to broadcast the evening news at dawn Beijing time. They would crowd around and watch everything we did. As long as we were getting their story out, they felt a measure of protection.

It was hard to believe a demonstration of this size could fail, especially when its goals were so modest. The students were calling for reform, not a revolution — more freedom of the press, a more open and representative government, a crackdown on corruption and curbs on inflation. From their mood, it seemed they would be satisfied with a simple statement of intent from the government.

We heard nothing, though, from the party leaders. They were all inside the Zhongnanhai, the former imperial compound where they lived just a few blocks from Tiananmen Square, with protesters camped outside its heavenly gates. It was clear from their silence that a power struggle was taking place, and as the days went on it became clear the hard-liners had the upper hand. The first sign was the coverage on Chinese TV. At first, it was sympathetic to the protesters. It even seemed the announcers and reporters were part of the movement. But after a few days the story changed and began emphasizing the "dangers" to the students. Doctors and nurses were interviewed about the health hazards of fasting, and living outdoors in such close quarters, without sanitation.

Then came a more ominous sign. They stopped interviewing the student leaders, and middle-aged protesters suddenly materialized on the nightly news, talking about overthrowing the government. Later I realized they were probably government agents, sent in to manufacture evidence of the "counter-revolutionary plot" the old guard was determined to crush.

At four a.m. on May 19, the communist leaders came out of their compound to "visit" the student leaders, camped out in a bus on the square. Li Peng, the leading hard-liner, walked briskly down the aisle, shaking hands perfunctorily with each of the students, not looking at them. He was followed by Zhao Ziyang, the party general-secretary, soon to be ousted and placed under house arrest. Zhao was nearly weeping as he took the students' hands in both of his. "We came too late," he told them. "We should have come before."

A few hours later in the square, we saw a half-dozen military helicopters coming over the horizon, flying low. "Get down," said our China correspondent John Sheahan. We were afraid they would open fire, with bullets or tear gas. In fact they just buzzed the perimeter of the square, flying over us as we huddled by our truck.

A short time later, loudspeakers crackled to life with a tinny female voice. It was the first official announcement we heard in the square.

Martial law has been declared in Beijing, she said, repeatedly. *The situation is very dangerous. Go home immediately.*

I ran to the typewriter and dashed off a news bulletin. After about three sentences I ripped it out and ran to Bettag, who met me with a rueful expression. "Never mind," he said, "They just pulled our plug."

We couldn't broadcast from the square any more, but CBS had its own satellite dish back at the hotel. We jumped into a van and peeled out. Almost immediately the driver slammed on the brakes, to avoid a protester sprinting across the road. We tumbled around in the van, then started up again, slower this time. The streets were filling with young people, setting up barricades. They waved us through.

Bettag was shouting over his mobile phone to New York, begging CBS to give up an hour of prime time for a special report that night. He had no luck, but it wouldn't have mattered if he did. When we got back to the hotel and rushed onto the air, we were interrupted by a delegation of Chinese officials, who said our permit had expired, and demanded we pull the plug on our own satellite. CBS broadcast that conversation live, but it ended with the Chinese having their way. Apparently CBS considered it quixotic to defy the government, even though millions of Chinese were willing to risk their lives doing just that. The company had been told, I heard, that it could never broadcast from China again unless we turned off the satellite and shut up. That, of course, assumed the communist regime would stay in power forever, which seemed unlikely at the time. I had the feeling we were capitulating too easily, but no one asked my opinion, and after a few minutes of gallant posturing, CBS gave in and Dan signed off. The lines went black, and there was nothing left to do but get out of town.

The next morning all roads out of Beijing were barricaded, and the scene at the airport was hysterical. Everyone with money, connections or a foreign passport was trying to leave before the shooting started. We fought our way through the mobs, carrying trunks full of videotape of the uprising. Customs could have seized the video, of course, but the agents were sympathetic to the protests. They waved us through. Twenty-four hours after martial law was declared in Beijing, I was sitting in the first-class cabin of a Pan Am jet, bound for Tokyo and New York, with a tray full of fancy food and wine. I felt like throwing up.

WHEN THE SHOOTING FINALLY BEGAN on a Saturday, two weeks later, I was at home. After listening to the radio for a few minutes, I turned it off, in denial and despair. I couldn't believe they were doing this — painting idealism as evil, crushing the best and bravest of their own children in the name of "stability."

Hundreds, maybe thousands, of young people were killed as the army moved in to retake the square. Some of them may have been among the students who met us every day, smiling and applauding, treating us as heroes there to protect them and show them the ways of freedom. Some may have been among the young people who came to our hotel, offering information and guidance. One student said he knew he could be ruining his future by talking to us in full view of the Chinese officials we had to deal with. "But I don't care," he said, in a quavering voice.

We left them all behind. When the attack came it was done in the dark, with no TV cameras present. The story got out, in still photographs and eyewitness accounts, but in such fragmentary form that no one was able to disprove the party line — that only a few people were killed as the army put down the vestiges of a "counter-revolutionary riot."

I felt like a coward, partly for myself — I was as happy as anyone to get out of Beijing — but also for CBS and the United States. Neither my employer nor my government felt capable of standing up for democracy. CBS could argue that it covered the story as best it could, and it wasn't its job to take sides. But the US government had no such excuse. The State Department offered only a string of lame, "even-handed" statements urging the two sides to settle their differences, as though both sides had equal moral standing.

In the square, the students had pestered us about rumors that President Bush would intervene to help them. We had to discourage them. Later, when that disembodied voice came over the loudspeakers, declaring martial law because of the "dangerous situation" in China, I had a flash on the true nature of history. In that instant it appeared to be what the Bible says it is — a fight to the finish between good and evil, truth and lies.

15

FISH FAMILY IN A BIG HOUSE

F ROM THE MID-1980S THROUGH THE EARLY '90S, on both sides
of my fiftieth birthday, things were going my way. I had a
great job and one adventure after another. Meanwhile I was
enjoying home and family. Debra was working part-time as the
family minister at Broadway Presbyterian Church. Most mornings I would take our three girls — Talitha, Cassia and Zoey —
to school at PS 87 on 78th Street, and sometimes stay for a
half-hour to help other kids learn to read. Then I'd walk to work
on 57th Street and spend the day writing the *CBS Evening
News*. Once or twice a month I'd follow up by running downtown to play my fiddle for a country dance. Family, work and
play all fit together like a puzzle, a pleasure to put together.

In those days PS 87 was one of the most admired schools
in the country, but not because of elevated test scores. Naomi
Hill, the principal, wasn't just interested in attracting the best
and brightest students — she wanted all kinds, all together. At
a parents meeting, one ambitious mother demanded to know
what the school offered for "gifted and talented" children. Ms.

Hill replied sweetly, "*All* our students are gifted and talented."

Rather than put the better-prepared (i.e., white, middle-class) students on a fast track, she organized the school so that kids of varying abilities and different ethnic groups were together in each classroom. The result was a lively, unpredictable environment where they learned to work together. There were Jews and Muslims, Blacks and Whites and Hispanics, and always new immigrants, from wherever in the world poverty, war or political turmoil was driving people to America. During the late '80s and early '90s one engine of immigration was the collapse of the Soviet empire. Cassia's best friend in fourth grade was Olga, who had just arrived from Ukraine and spoke no English. Cassia helped her learn the language — she was completely fluent after one year — and Olga, a Soviet-trained dancer, brought her to the School of American Ballet. Two years later they were toy soldiers in New York City Ballet's *Nutcracker*.

At PS 87, parents were part of the show, bringing in their talents to supplement the teachers. Debra called square dances in music class. Once or twice a week I would stay to help immigrant children learn to read. One of my students was a Dominican kid who spoke Spanish at home. Thinking to connect with Hispanic culture, I brought in a book my mother read me at his age, *Ferdinand the Bull*. Ferdinand is a gentle, friendly beast, and when they take him to the bull ring in Madrid, all he wants to do is smell the flowers in the ladies' hair. This drives the matadors, the picadors and the banderilleros crazy, but nothing they do will make Ferdinand fight. So they send him back home to smell the flowers.

My little student Hector read dutifully through this children's classic. When he finished, I asked him how he liked the book. To my surprise, he curled his lip with the contempt of a matador for a cowardly bull.

"Stupid," was all he said.

So I learned something at PS 87, revising my opinion of *Ferdinand the Bull*. It's charmingly written and illustrated, but to a Hispanic boy, its universal message is bull.

Fortunately, at PS 87 kids didn't learn English just from books chosen by well-intentioned adults. One day Talitha came home from kindergarten and announced solemnly, "Daddy, I have *wroten* a book."

Starting at four or five, kids were authors of their own works, bound and published in class. Talitha's first book was about her two pet ants. One was dead, which made her sad. But the other was still alive.

Zoey, in kindergarten, wrote about a young pumpkin, *The Papkn*. Sometimes he was scared, sometimes he was bored, sometimes he was sad. One day he spilled his milk. His mother "got a spag and wapt it up." He was embarrassed! This was illustrated with a misshapen, miserable pumpkin. But it had a happy ending — after the milk accident "the rest of his laf it was grat." As an English schoolboy I was horrified at first by invented spellings, but I came to love them because you could see a kid's mind at work, on the right track.

Cassia wrote a book when Debra's father died, her first experience of death. Seeing her withdrawn and sad, the kindergarten teacher took her aside and helped her compose her thoughts. The book was *My Grandpa Died*. It told how "Pop" would take the girls riding on his lawnmower. It described Cassie's last visit with him in the hospital, in bed with tubes in him. The ending was a simple account of loss: "Now I have two grandmas, and no grandpas."

After the cultural and intellectual ferment of PS 87, I spent the rest of the day in the CBS newsroom, where the atmosphere seemed bland by comparison. Writing for Dan Rather was much easier than for Walter Cronkite. Dan generally left the writers alone and trusted what we did. But write what we would, the results on the air were unpredictable. Dan became famous for his blank spots and bizarre ad-libs.

One day I wrote a short item about the newly discovered health benefits of dark beer. Dan read it flawlessly, except for one little word. He called it "dank beer."

Dank beer! I crumpled to the floor behind the desk, afraid I had committed a typo that made him look like a fool. But no, my fellow writer Paul Fischer pulled me up.

— It wasn't you, he said, you wrote it right.

Dan was just reading the script on the teleprompter and somehow came up with "dank beer." What was he thinking? Only Dan could say, but no one dared ask him. The executive producer delicately told him he had "misspoken," and they corrected it for the taped edition of the broadcast.

Dan often ad-libbed his closing line, especially on holidays. One St. Patrick's Day, he signed off with "This is Danny O'Rather reporting." But another St. Patrick's Day his mind wandered, and he stared into the camera. He knew it was a holiday, but which one? After a split second, he blurted out: "Happy Thanksgiving."

Trying to eclipse the memory of Walter Cronkite, Dan wanted to come up with a signature sign-off that would top Walter's famous "That's the way it is." He went away to meditate on some mountaintop, and came back with one word: "Courage." This was how he wanted to say good night to the nation.

The nation, unanimously, hated it. CBS management begged him not to say it. The writers wouldn't write it. But the anchorman's ultimate power is that on live TV, what comes out of his mouth is up to him. Every night for a week we prayed he would just say good night, but he kept at it: "Courage." Finally he yielded to popular demand, and just said good night.

Courage was Dan's calling card. He had fought his way onto the network news as a local reporter in Texas, covering a hurricane that everyone else fled. He did this again and again for decades, driving into the storm as everyone else evacuated. In the end it became a strange sight, a gray-haired man in his sixties defying nature. When Hurricane Opal struck in 1995, Dan stood near the Gulf Coast in 140-mph winds, his hair blowing wildly, his cheeks distended. He had little to say except, "This is what it's like to be in winds of 140 miles an hour!" Off camera, a producer was flat on the ground, hugging Dan's ankles to keep him from blowing away.

Dan's problem was that he didn't have much to say. Still, he wanted to be at the center of things, the anchorman the nation turned to in times of trial. He got by with courage, plus incredible good looks — a female colleague of mine said she got aroused every time she saw him on the screen — and a deep, sonorous voice that made him sound authoritative.

He needed writers. The one big story I missed in 1989 was the fall of the Berlin Wall. I was feeling tired that day and had gone home for a nap at lunch time when the story broke. By the time I got back, the train was leaving the station — Bettag and Rather were off to Germany with an entourage that didn't include a writer. Forced to ad-lib the whole story, Dan wound up standing by the wall as the Germans came together, saying again and again, "What's happening here is indescribable!"

That conveyed his enthusiasm, but nothing more. Dan didn't know enough about history to compose any eloquent thoughts. From then on, I made it clear to Bettag that as the foreign writer I wanted to go along, wherever in the world they went.

IN ALL MY LIFE, JUST TWO WORK PLACES felt like home to me — the writers' desk at the *CBS Evening News,* and the fiddler's chair at the English country dance in Greenwich Village.

I discovered country dancing in the '70s, while working on the Cronkite show. It probably saved me from an alcoholic depression — a common fate among Cronkite's staff. The working day was excruciatingly tense, and I felt drained by the end. I'd head downtown and eat dinner at my favorite restaurant, a tiny counter on Greenwich Avenue, Chez Brigitte. Brigitte's *cuisine soignée* was the closest thing I got to love in those bitter years of working and divorcing. After dinner I'd walk in the Village, then go home, drink until I was half-numb, meditate for a few minutes and crawl into bed, a futon on the floor. Sometimes I felt like Gregor Samsa in Kafka's "Metamorphosis."

One summer night, walking on Greenwich Avenue a block from Brigitte's, I saw folk-dancing in a school playground, and stayed to watch. They did Balkan and Israeli line dances, Scandinavian couple dances, and something else that caught my fancy. It was an English dance called "Hole in the Wall," in longways formation, with couples moving up and down the set, casting outward and walking up the middle hand in hand. I could do that, I thought.

The dance was free and open to all, so one night I walked through the playground gate, found a partner and joined in "Hole in the Wall." It felt natural, a walking version of the manners I'd seen as an English schoolboy. After that I stayed for another dance, an American contra that had the same formation and some of the same figures, but was more bouncy and lively. I could do that, too.

The teacher said he learned these dances from the Country Dance and Song Society, which held its own dances in the Village. So that fall, I found my way to a church basement on Thirteenth Street, and discovered my people. They were mostly young and intellectual, but with a physical side that needed some easy release. They did English and American dances, taught by ladies from England who reminded me of my school teachers. Genny Shimer in particular was authoritative but thoroughly democratic, interested in everyone. She took a liking to me, and eventually mentored me as I learned to teach English dances myself.

I danced for a couple of years before I brought my fiddle and asked to sit in with the band. Many of the tunes were familiar from my English school days, like "The Curly-headed Ploughboy," or "My Love She's but a Lassie." They just spun out of the fiddle as if they were stored there.

Many of the American tunes were also familiar. I played classical violin as a child, but started fiddling in college when some of my folk-singing friends got up a bluegrass band. At CDSS I got to work on both styles.

I still needed some help with American fiddling, and eventually found a partner to learn from. Bill Christophersen was a New York fiddler who had picked up the old-time Appalachian style. He lived near us in Morningside Heights and we traded tunes at a weekly session on 113th Street. All the local folk musicians showed up there. Eventually we formed a band that met at our house — Debra on piano, Bill and I on fiddles, and

Vicky Gould on accordion. We called ourselves the Fish Family. The name came from Talitha, three years old, who showed us a painting she made of red, blue and yellow blobs. What was it?

"A fish family in a great big house."

The Fish Family was New York's first contra-dance band. We played our first dance at the Church in the Village in 1981, and recorded our first album, "Fluke Hits," in our living room in 1987. Debra was our secret weapon. Her piano playing was modest, just rhythm with no frills, but she had a bounce on the off-beat that gave the whole mix a dancing lilt.

We lost our piano player after our third child was born. But the Fish Family is still playing gigs in 2015, piecing together a pickup band around our twin fiddles. Bill and I get together once a week to trade tunes, and even write some, trading lines as we sit across from each other in the living room, or outdoors on the Columbia campus in summer.

We have plenty to talk about between tunes. Like me, Bill is an English major, a teacher, journalist, editor and critic. He's also a poet. We'll just go on about ordinary stuff, and Whitman or Keats or Mark Twain will show up in the conversation. Such company is rare, it makes me happy.

16

THE AFRICAN EXPLORER

ONE MORNING IN 1990, while things were going my way, I was walking down West 57th Street to the CBS Broadcast Center, wondering if there was anything more I could do to make my life complete. One wish occurred — to see South Africa.

I walked into the lobby and a producer ran up to me. He said, "Can you go to South Africa, tomorrow?"

THE STORY WAS THAT NELSON MANDELA was about to be released from prison after twenty-eight years, the climax of negotiations between the white-minority government and Mandela's African National Congress. We flew overnight to London and then to Johannesburg, then to Cape Town where he was supposed to be freed, then back to Johannesburg, because the plan had changed. It changed several more times in the next two days, until it was finally settled that he would appear at a soccer stadium in Soweto, the black township outside Johannesburg. By then I had my first impressions of Africa, from the air and the road — warm and dusty, reddish-brown, with wild, lush foliage.

The stadium held eighty-five thousand people, and it was full when we got there, with more coming in. They had streamed from all around Johannesburg, walking, jogging, dancing and singing, crowding onto every available vehicle until trucks looked like trees festooned with people.

Mandela was more than an hour late, but no one was bored. The crowd made up a song and sang it as a call and response: One side of the stadium would sing high, NEL-SON MANDELAH! The other side would answer low, NEL-SON MANDELAH!

South Africa's white police kept their distance, sitting in cars outside the stadium, looking tense and surly. Security inside was provided by "ANC Marshals," teenage boys who frisked everyone for weapons, and tried to keep the crowds moving. Foolishly, I left the CBS News group to look for a vantage point among the people, and came close to dying on the job. A crowd was squeezed into a passageway blocked by people on both ends, and I felt the air being forced out of my lungs. Then somehow the pressure eased and we began to move. I found a place in the upper deck behind two of the very few white people in the crowd – a couple of middle-aged Anglican priests in their vestments.

Finally, Mandela appeared. A convoy of vehicles drove onto the track around the soccer field, and he emerged, waving. He looked nothing like the thirty-year-old photographs we knew, but it was him — slim and erect, calm and disciplined, ready to take up his role as leader of South Africa's black majority. But where would he lead them?

Apartheid was still in force — housing, education, employment, health care all divided by race, with blacks getting the worst of everything. In freeing Mandela, the government had committed itself to dismantling the racist system, but it had to be held to its word. In this first speech following his release, Mandela laid out the terms of what would be a near-miraculous peaceful transition to majority rule.

OVER YEARS OF NEGOTIATION IN PRISON, Mandela had refused to renounce violence, and he repeated that refusal to the crowd in Soweto. He said the ANC would "pursue its armed struggle against the government as long as the violence of apartheid continues." But the body and soul of the speech was a call for peace. The ANC, he said, is as opposed to black domination as white domination. Sternly warning his people against violence, he said if there was any fighting to be done, the ANC would handle it. The people's job was to show their good will, to demonstrate to whites that a South Africa without apartheid would be a "better home for all."

Mandela spoke for about half an hour, but most in the crowd were too excited to listen carefully. They applauded his calls for decent housing, better education and a living wage for black workers. Still, there was a buzz of conversation in the stadium throughout. A CBS correspondent told me he thought the speech was a flop. I disagreed. Maybe the crowd would have been more excited if he called for revenge, but the results would have been disastrous. They seemed happy enough with his message of peace and reconciliation.

After Mandela spoke, the entire crowd stood up and sang the unofficial national anthem of South Africa, *Nkoze Sikelele Africa*. Mandela and his wife Winnie stood side by side, right fists raised in the black power salute. In the upper deck, the

Anglican priests joined in the same song and salute.

Mandela made his position unmistakable the next day, when we interviewed him at home in Soweto. Looking for emotion and conflict, Dan Rather asked him what his worst experience was in prison. The man who had suffered torture, isolation, injury and disease for decades, answered firmly and promptly, "I don't remember." He claimed to have a great ability to forget unpleasant things, and so remembered nothing negative from all those years.

MANDELA'S RELEASE WAS ANOTHER VISION of the then-current view of history, that it was all headed for a happy ending with the triumph of liberal democracy everywhere. But another vision made its appearance a couple of years later, in another part of Africa. My last adventure with CBS News was in December 1992, when President Bush sent the U.S. Marines into Somalia.

This was another impromptu scramble for us — an overnight flight to London, from there to Nairobi and then a flight with a bush pilot into Somalia, in an overloaded small plane. The last item aboard was a case of beer the pilot said had to go in the back, or we wouldn't get off the ground.

We got there a few days ahead of the Marines. The U.S. military was going in to relieve a famine in Somalia – a famine that had more to do with politics than crop failure. Relief organizations had sent plenty of food, but it wasn't reaching the starving people in the interior. Somalia had no central government. It had been a pawn in the cold war, switching sides between the U.S. and the Soviet Union. Now, the Soviet Union was defunct, and the United States had no strategic interests in the region. So the country had reverted to clan warfare, and starvation was a common strategy in African civil wars. The

Marines' mission was to provide secure corridors for the relief shipments.

CBS was going in pursuit of a story. For more than a year we'd seen pictures of starving Somali children, but there had been no talk of a rescue mission. That changed shortly after George H.W. Bush lost his bid for re-election, and was left with nothing to do until January 20th, when Bill Clinton would be sworn in. Contemporary accounts said he fell into depression, until he came up with an idea to flesh out his vision of a New World Order, now that the U.S. was the only superpower. A month after his defeat, he was reportedly energized by the idea of riding to the rescue in Somalia, righting an egregious wrong, doing the "Lord's work."

Our idea was to grab the TV audience with a story that would wrench their guts and warm their hearts. Somalia was a natural — America using its awesome military power for good, feeding the hungry, healing the sick, building a new nation in the ruins of war.

"Ruins" was no exaggeration. We landed at the Mogadishu airport with no lights or communication with the ground. The control tower was empty – trashed and looted like every other public facility in the capital. On the tarmac, we were met by gunmen demanding a "landing fee." This was the faction in control of the airport. A small force of U.N. peacekeepers from Pakistan was supposed to be in charge, but they were outgunned, holed up in their tents and bunkers on the airport perimeter, refusing to come out for anyone.

CBS News had made connections, so we were driven to a rented villa near the city center, steering around huge craters in the streets. These private residences had their own power generators and security squads, inside walls topped by shards of broken glass. Young men and boys with machine guns hung around the compound and prowled the streets. Somalia was awash in American and Soviet weapons, left over from its years as a cold-war client state.

Setting out to cover the story, we drove inland and found children dying by the roadsides, too weak to beg for food. We interviewed the head of the "interim government," just one of the factions fighting for control in Mogadishu. He said bringing peace and unity to Somalia was his "dream." Meanwhile his interim government was blocking food shipments to the interior. We talked to another warlord, whose forces controlled the port of Kismayu. Dan Rather returned from the interview shaking his head. "That man is a stone killer," he said.

Things would change, we figured, when the Marines arrived.

The invasion had all the trappings of an amphibious assault — submarines and hovercraft leading the way for troop carriers, with helicopter gunships circling overhead. It was an impressive show of force, but there was no one to resist it. The Marines swarmed ashore at dawn, and grabbed a homeless Somali sleeping in an airport outbuilding. They threw him to the ground, pointed guns at his head and screamed in English, "Don't move!"

Screaming at Somalis in English, at gunpoint, turned out to be the Marines' way of dealing with the people they came to rescue. In a country of armed, ruthless bullies, they set out to be the best-armed and most ruthless. Some of them groused openly about the charitable goals of their mission. "I didn't sign up for the Peace Corps," said one.

The mission succeeded in its initial goal of allowing grain shipments to move out of the port. But its long-term failure seemed assured from the beginning. US troops could serve as a police force to keep the clans and factions from open warfare. But they couldn't make peace in Somalia. All they could do was make enemies.

The end result is well known. Less than a year after US troops came in, Somalis shot down an Army Blackhawk helicopter and killed the crew, along with troops who tried to rescue them. Mobs then dragged the Americans' bodies through the streets of Mogadishu, celebrating. President Clinton pulled American troops out. Somalia was left to fend for itself, written off as the first of many "failed states" in the post-cold war era.

SOMALIA WAS ALSO THE LAST of the *CBS Evening News*'s impromptu flights to unlikely places. Once the nation's most trusted source of news, the broadcast was cutting back its scope. With growing competition from cable news and the internet, the audience was shrinking every year. Revenues fell and costs had to be cut. Foreign news was the first casualty. Under pressure, the news division closed bureaus, fired correspondents, and grounded the airborne anchor desk.

Bettag was fired in 1991, when he refused to go along with the cost-cutting regime. He was replaced by Erik Sorenson, a new-age corporate type from Los Angeles, who had radically different ideas about everything.

Starting with the décor: Sorenson replaced the Japanese prints in Bettag's office with a life-size cutout photograph of basketball player Michael Jordan. He emptied the bookshelves, replacing his predecessor's library with just a few skinny volumes — one about golf, another on chiropractic medicine, and a biography of H. Ross Perot, whose presidential campaign we would soon be covering with a positive tilt.

In his first staff meeting, Sorenson announced a sea-change in the *CBS Evening News*. No longer would it be the "broadcast of record," i.e. we were no longer obliged to cover every important story of the day. Rather than put on a TV show for people who like news, he said we could now create a news show for "people who like TV." In practice, that was a few minutes of hard news at the top, followed by a parade of stories designed to titillate or terrify. Sorenson was especially keen on stories about children being kidnapped or murdered. Our own children were in grade school at the time, and after they were duly terrified by a few of these reports, Debra banned the Evening News at home.

My father said he liked being a journalist because he never had to do anything he was ashamed of. Now I was working on a product that wasn't fit for my own family, and I was ashamed.

IT WAS A LONG FOUR YEARS, but I managed to outlast Sorenson, whose formula brought a further decline in the ratings, and scathing reviews in the press. The broadcast regained some of its credibility under his successors, Andrew Heyward and Jeff Fager. Still, the amount of time devoted to news kept shrinking, a few seconds at a time, replaced by commercials and self-promotion within the show. They added headlines at the top, with hyped-up background music, plus "teases" before each commercial break. In 1996 I reluctantly accepted a promotion to news editor, for a second tour of duty on the hot seat. By then the job had been stripped of its authority, involved more writing than editing, and felt more like advertising than journalism.

The final indignity, for me, was the addition of ten-second promos for local stations, to go out at 5:50, forty minutes before airtime. Fager pressed me relentlessly to come up with cute, uninformative lines that would supposedly make the *Evening News* essential viewing. Besides being journalistically worthless, this had to be done in late afternoon, just as the *Evening News* was taking shape. It took the writers away from their real work just as the crunch was coming.

Then the promos started to multiply. They wanted one for New York, one for LA, then Chicago, Pittsburgh, and on and on, including greetings to the anchors in each market. "Hi, Wendy and Mitch. On the *Evening News* tonight, the story of a young man who refused to give up his American Dream!"

Why "American Dream?" That was just one of the features that became part of the *Evening News* in the nineties — special sections paid for by sponsors, in this case Fidelity Investments, which would help you realize your American Dream. These segments took another huge bite out of the time available for real news. They could not be postponed, cut, or even moved from their reserved place in the lineup, no matter what else was happening. And they had to be promoted, relentlessly.

I cursed, I complained, and on top of that I was no good at writing promo copy. I couldn't get over the instinct to impart information, when the idea was to raise questions and leave them hanging. Eventually they let the writers off the hook, and producers took over the promo-writing duties. But I paid the price for my un-cooperation.

CBS News had been through a series of cutbacks and purges in my time, and I had survived. Fired once, I came back and stayed for more than a decade, until I felt like a fixture on the *Evening News*. I counted on working until sixty-five or so, then retiring on my own terms. So I mostly failed to notice the signs that were going up in the nineties, for example signs that my sharply-worded dissenting opinions were no longer appreciated by my bosses. I had little respect for the younger people now in charge. But I didn't appreciate how little respect they had for me.

I lasted until the year 2000, when I was fifty-eight. A new boss called me in one Friday after the show, and with no ceremony, told me they weren't going to renew my contract.

— Your heart just isn't in it any more, he said.

I couldn't argue.

I stumbled out of the building, walked to the subway and took the wrong train, going downtown instead of up. An hour later I came home, and shaking, told my wife and daughters I'd lost my job. I felt as if my moorings had been cut, and I was floating, detached from the world.

17

A LITTLE LEAR

WHEN I WAS A BOY, I often heard my father call himself a "failure." He said this in a bitter, self-despising tone, as if it were his fault he wasn't a world-honored journalist. He would compare himself disparagingly with men he'd gone to school with — Clifton Daniel, the managing editor of the New York Times, or the columnist James Reston. To hear him tell it, there was no reason why he shouldn't be as celebrated as they were, instead of an obscure editor at the Associated Press. He beat himself up continually, judging himself by the standard of some committee handing out prizes for journalistic excellence. For him, no other standard existed. Men were judged by their prominence in their chosen field.

Listening to him carry on this way, I made a vow never to go down that path, never call myself a failure. In this way I hoped to be his opposite. But unwittingly I set myself up for the same fate, because I accepted his standard. I would judge myself as the world judged me, by my prominence. The difference was, I expected to succeed.

In real life, though, "success" is rare. A few people are honored time and again for their outstanding labors, and end their careers with testimonial dinners. But most blunder about, winning some and losing some, and end with a loss or a losing streak. If they're lucky, they get out with a comfortable retirement, which they spend fading from the world's memory.

Pop won a few, lost more, judged himself a failure, and died at fifty-eight, before he even had a chance to retire. At fifty-eight, I got fired for the second and last time from the *CBS Evening News*. When I came home in disarray that night, seventeen-year-old Talitha looked at me wide-eyed and said, "What are you gonna do?"

It took some weeks to come up with an answer, but eventually it was that, having "failed," I would not accept my status; I would reverse it as fast as possible. And so I set out to turn failure into success. My first notion was to go into print journalism, which I'd always felt was my true calling. I had gotten into broadcasting by accident, and though I liked it, felt there was more room for my talents in newspapers, magazines, and books. My brother Angus made a good living and enjoyed himself as a sportswriter and columnist for the *Washington Post*. If he could thrive in print journalism, I could certainly do the same.

I answered an ad for a copy editor at a financial magazine, and had a nice chat with the editor, a young woman who seemed impressed with my credentials. She handed me the copy-editing test they gave to all applicants, and told me there was no one way to do it — just use my skills and instincts to make it a better magazine story.

Supremely confident in my editing, I grabbed the test with relish. But as I started in, I found this wasn't exactly the work

I was used to, and was uncertain what to do. I wound up cutting a lot of words and phrases, making it shorter but not necessarily better. Still, I thought my natural charm and talent would shine through in the hiring process, and expected to hear back from the editor within days. She didn't call me, so I called her. They'd found somebody else.

The Reuters news agency was extremely flattering in reply to my query about employment. We would certainly be interested in a person with such experience, wrote the director of personnel. That was the last I heard from them.

After a few such disappointments, I shifted my comeback plan to a field where I knew I could stand out — teaching. The NYU Department of Journalism was effusive in praising my resume, but they too found someone else.

Daunted, I decided to drop my ambitions a notch and go back to my very first plan, back when I just got out of college. I could be a teacher of English to adoring pupils in some elite private high school. Offering myself as God's gift to elite private schooling, I got in return repeated, rude rebuffs. It seems private schools have certain criteria for hiring new teachers, and they weren't about to waive their standards, no matter how much I waved mine. My only offer was for a part-time, temporary position in a middle school my sons had attended in New Jersey. But I was too proud to start at the bottom.

About this time I began to sit for hours in an easy chair at home, waiting for an impulse that never quite took shape. I was humiliated when twelve-year-old Zoey came home from school and asked me, "What do you do all day?"

It was time for a radical re-think. I racked my brains for something I'd be good at — something that suited my talents, but I'd never had time to pursue. Soon a gem of an answer appeared — Shakespearean acting! I loved Shakespeare, had read or seen most of the plays, and could speak Elizabethan English fluently, if not accurately. An actress friend of mine encouraged me. She'd been around the New York theater scene for decades, had performed on Broadway, and said, "Sure, go ahead. In two weeks, you'll be in *King Lear*."

Two weeks later, I was in *King Lear!*

Visions of glory danced in my head as I made my way downtown to begin rehearsals for the role of Gloucester, the king's loyal friend, father of the hero Edgar and the arch-villain Edmund. I landed the part at my first audition, which I attended with at least a hundred other hopefuls, at the American Theater of Actors on West 54th Street.

My actress friend wasn't at all surprised when she heard of my success, which she had predicted. Shakespeare plays are constantly being produced at every level in New York, and they need men of a certain age to play the roles of kings, dukes, archbishops, doting fathers and ancient pistols. Young actors are as plentiful as pigeons, but the 58-year-olds have mostly given up. And a professional 58-year-old wouldn't be caught dead at the American Theater of Actors.

ATA didn't pay, but that was standard for off-off-Broadway theaters. This company didn't even supply the actors with a script, telling them to bring their own, without specifying which edition. This sometimes made for interesting rehearsals, with actors arguing about who says what. They did have a large supply of old costumes, issued dirty and in need of repair. Shoes and tights were supplied by the actors, which again made for some interesting contrasts.

The stage for this midsummer night's production was a platform behind a theatrical office building, with two long benches for the public. Rats lived under the platform, and sometimes made an entrance if they smelled food. The place was owned by the director of ATA, James Jennings, who made money renting out three theaters in the building, and amused himself by putting on Shakespeare in the rear.

As director, Jennings had nothing to say about the play or the characters, leaving it to each actor to interpret. He did know how to keep a show moving, and get it in under three hours. Once we had it down, he just served as lighting director. He would turn on one big light to start the show, turn it off at intermission, then on again for the second half. After the first few performances, he would just turn on the light, go upstairs to his office, come back for intermission, and repeat.

Actors also had to supply the audience. Jennings did nothing to publicize his Shakespeare festival, except type up flyers with the names of the cast. These we spread among family, friends, and neighbors. On our best nights we had forty or fifty spectators, but more often the cast outnumbered the audience. One evening five people showed up, including a family of four with a ten-year-old boy, who entertained himself by rolling back and forth the length of the bench on his skateboard. The family left at intermission, so for the second half we strutted and fretted before an audience of one. He was a friend of one of the actresses, and happened to be a famous economist, William Seidman, whom I recognized from his appearances on TV. Seidman had come to several performances, and chatted with the actors after the show. He was a class act himself, the hero of the evening. After watching the second half all alone, he leaped up and gave us a full-length, standing ovation.

ATA's *Lear* could be a humbling experience for an actor, but I loved my role. All I had to do to feel my way into it was to imagine the old CBS newsroom under Walter Cronkite. That was "The King and his Court." Gloucester is one of the able vassals who owe their success to the King, and repay him with utter loyalty. As his friend Kent says to the deluded Lear, who's threatening to have him killed, "My life I never held but as a pawn to wage against thine enemies."

I had problems playing that role at CBS, but could imagine myself in it on stage. What is Gloucester but a little Lear, an old man ruined, trying to bear up under the worst, even when his eyes are gouged out by the vicious Cornwall? I loved screaming in the eye-gouging scene, and diving off the platform when the blind Gloucester thinks he's jumping off the Cliffs of Dover. But my favorite scene of all was in Act Four, when Lear and I sit hopeless on the moor, as in *Waiting for Godot*. The King is mad, I say, why am I still torturing myself with the truth?

> . . .*How stiff is my vile sense*
> *That I stand up, and have ingenious feeling*
> *Of my huge sorrows! Better I were distract;*
> *So should my thoughts be severed from my griefs,*
> *And woes by wrong imaginations lose*
> *The knowledge of themselves.*

ACTING WAS A DISTRACTION FOR ME, a way of severing my thoughts from my griefs. I had sustained the devastating loss of my prominence in the world, and didn't even want to think about it. How much better to put on a costume and become someone else, whose trials could be played out for a brief hour on the stage. My final favorite moment was the curtain call, when I'd run out waving the bloody bandage that had covered my eyes. See, I'm not blind, not dead, just a player who can make you believe these things. (I copied this flourish from an actor in the Greek National Theater, playing Oedipus the King.)

Being an actor itself was another layer of unreality. I didn't really believe I was bound for a brilliant career on the stage, but I could pretend to believe it, as long as I had a part. Actors all entertain themselves by imagining this role, or the next, will be their breakthrough. They're happy as long as the illusion lasts.

FOR ME, IT LASTED ABOUT TWO YEARS. I performed in half-a-dozen Shakespeare plays with entry-level troupes. But gradually it became clear I would never make a penny as an actor. No examples came to mind of a sixty-year-old novice vaulting to prominence in the theater.

Instead I needed to face my own sorrows, and find a way to act out my own life.

18

THE CUP OF TREMBLING

B Y THIS TIME DEBRA AND I had switched roles. She was the breadwinner, commuting to the Presbyterian Church in Leonia, New Jersey, where she was the solo pastor, her first full-time job in ministry. I was the stay-at-home father to three teenage daughters. I cooked, which I enjoyed, and cleaned the house, which I didn't. And being depressed, I wasn't much help to the girls.

Talitha was OK with it. She was seventeen when I lost my job, and independent for her age. She sympathized, and didn't ask for much. The next year she went off to college, where she had to battle with her own loneliness and anxiety. Like me she took refuge in music, learning to play the bass, and performing with her guitar as a singer-songwriter.

Cassia, at fifteen, tried to protect me from my miseries. She didn't want me to read *Sister Carrie*, worrying that I would see myself in the character of Hurstwood — unemployed, depressed, in a terminal decline. It made me wince to think she saw me that way.

Zoey was twelve when her world fell apart. Her father lost his job and her mother went off to work just as she was going though middle school and puberty. She always had a lively mind and I loved talking with her, but I understood little of her inner turmoils, and never appreciated her circus arts the way I did Cassie's ballet, or Talitha's folk music and dance. And being self-centered, I didn't try to hide or soften my preferences.

Zoey developed a terrible eating disorder that wrecked her life for years. For years I stood by, feeling there was little I could do, because I couldn't understand or identify with this bizarre ailment. Finally my own psychotherapist shamed me into trying to understand. Slowly, I came to realize that my detachment was part of the problem. It was the other side of my attachment to my own concerns, my refusal to share in someone else's suffering. Zoey let me have it on multiple occasions, often in the presence of her own therapists. In the end I had no choice but to accept that being a father means not just standing around kibitzing, but understanding what your child is feeling, taking her hand and going through it together. I didn't want to go there, but Zoey made me, and I'm grateful for it.

MEANWHILE I HAD TO DO SOMETHING with my days. I had always looked down on volunteer work — that was for housewives and losers. But now that I was both, why not? Debra kept suggesting opportunities for service, volunteer work I might enjoy. Finally I decided to apply for a job where I knew they wouldn't refuse — the soup kitchen at our old church, Broadway Presbyterian.

I called the director, my friend Chris Fay, and he said I could come in anytime, and do whatever I wanted. In short order, I found my niche in that business — dishing up lunches and fitting four of them on a tray that was slightly too small for four plates. The soup kitchen served hundreds of poor and homeless people every week, and I and a co-worker were in charge of estimating the crowd and matching it to the number of plates. My partner was Bob, a part-time professor of political science at Columbia. He'd been raised by communists to prepare the way for the revolution, judging by his quotes from Lenin, Mao and Chou En-lai. He didn't seem to believe in communist ideology any more, and didn't believe in religion either, but couldn't break the habit of identifying with the poor and oppressed.

Bob was an essential part of the soup kitchen staff. Many of the other volunteers were homeless themselves, and most of them were mentally ill, poorly educated or illiterate. Bob was the smartest guy in the room — the only one who could count the crowd, divide it by four, and come up with the right number of trays. I couldn't do it myself.

DEBRA ALSO SHOWED ME AN ITEM in the School of American Ballet newsletter that Cassie brought home. SAB needed tutors for foreign students attending public schools in New York. These kids spent most of their time in the dance studio, and their heavy work load plus the language barrier made school difficult, if not impossible. So I signed up to help them with their homework. I spent hours every week with dancers from Asia and Latin America, explaining US history, reading *Macbeth* out loud, smuggling in Cliff Notes for a Korean boy who didn't have time to read *Les Misérables*.

Two girls from Latin America were struggling with James Baldwin's story of the ghetto, "Sonny's Blues." So we read it aloud, tracing the emotions of two brothers as they move through the menacing atmosphere of 1950s Harlem. At the end Sonny, just out of prison and on shaky ground, is in a bar playing piano with some of his old jazz buddies. He struggles, then hits his stride on a blues. His brother orders him a drink, and the waitress brings a scotch and milk. Sonny puts it by the piano where it vibrates with the sound. Baldwin describes it as "the very cup of trembling."

What a strange ending, we all thought, but somehow moving. Why scotch and milk? I never heard of such a drink. But milk is good for you, and scotch is dangerous. They're like the good and bad of life, mixed together in one nourishing, intoxicating brew.

And what is the "cup of trembling"? We began to talk about ballet. When you rise in a full arabesque, every muscle in your body is tense, pushing to its limit. But inside you're soft, vibrating with the music. One of the girls was living on the edge in New York, with no money or family, lost in school, lacking the right papers to stay in America. But she was a gorgeous, powerful dancer. "Yes," she said softly. "It's the very cup of trembling." She wrote a paper using that line, and got a good mark for a change.

BALLET, FOR ME, was the road not taken. By the time it diverged from my path, it was too late to take it. But I wandered onto it anyway, repeatedly.

Grinnell had a modern dance group, and I had joined it on a lark with a couple of other sophomores, Bennett Bean and Phil Balick. We were the only men in the group. I enjoyed leaping around and grappling with nubile young women, but wasn't too serious about it.

Then one weekend, the Canadian National Ballet came to

perform at the college. I didn't expect to like it — the only ballets I'd seen, on TV, looked old-fashioned and stilted. I went as a dancer, out of curiosity.

First on the program was *Concerto Barocco,* to Bach's "Concerto for Two Violins." The ballet was by George Balanchine, described in the program as a leading contemporary choreographer.

The music began. Following the first violin line, a Russian ballerina stepped out onto her pointed toe, unfolding her other leg into the air. Her arched foot soared, even as she was falling forward, then running. A second ballerina stepped out, dancing against the second violin part. By the end of *Concerto Barocco,* my views on ballet had changed completely. This was music made visible, in the flesh.

Another Balanchine ballet, to Tchaikovsky's "Serenade for Strings," left my liberal arts education in ruins. We'd been taught to divide the arts into classical, romantic and modern eras, each with its own distinctive style and values. But *Serenade* was all of these, and more. It was a love story, a Greek myth, an abstraction, a revelation. I wrote a column for the school paper, raving about Balanchine's art.

AFTER GRADUATING AND MOVING to New York, I went to see Balanchine's New York City Ballet at Lincoln Center, in 1965. And shortly after that I tiptoed into a Ballet Fundamentals class at the New Dance Group Studio on 46th Street, in my first pair of ballet slippers. I'd learned to wear tights, but this was embarrassing. Then I saw that the shoes were part of the aesthetic — the arched foot and extended fingers were the outer reaches of the human body, pointing beyond itself.

The extreme turnout of the feet allowed the body to move

fluidly in any direction. And the turnout of the hips and thighs made the center of the body not just more mobile, but more visible, more expressive. Ballet caught my imagination like no other performing art. This was meditation in action — the whole body, the whole self as an instrument.

Unfortunately, it was ten years too late to even think about becoming a ballet dancer. It's a discipline that has to be practiced while the body is still growing, still taking shape. At twenty-three, I couldn't force my feet into a fully turned-out fifth position without wrecking my knees and hips. Besides that, I had a wife, a child, and a career.

Nonetheless, I couldn't let it go. I took two or three ballet classes a week, and thought about it continually. I became a balletomane, hanging around Lincoln Center in the days when ballet was a cheap ticket, following New York City Ballet and American Ballet Theater, as well as the Royal Ballet and other visiting troupes. And I even got to perform, for a couple of nights.

New Dance Group was mainly a modern dance school. But Celene Keller, the head ballet teacher, was hoping to make a name for herself as a choreographer, so she decided to put on a Ballet Workshop in 1966. For this she recruited dozens of young dancers, mostly from the School of American Ballet. Like most choreographers she was short of "boys" to partner the girls, so she plucked them out of her classes at New Dance Group. I was easy to recruit, even though I had too many other things to do, and barely had learned the basics of ballet.

Celene gave me about half an hour of instruction in partnering, and cast me in the *corps de ballet* of her pickup company, which cost me many weekends for rehearsals, away from home while Mary Jo was pregnant with our second child. I struggled with some of the steps, but Celene taught us tricks of the trade. Those of us who couldn't do a double pirouette would turn once, then wiggle our heads to look like we were still spinning.

My main job was to elevate a willowy fourteen-year-old as she leaped, steady her as she turned, and lift her on my shoulder in the finale. I could just handle these basic tasks, and managed to get through the two performances. My wife and two-year-old daughter Jenny came to watch, along with my parents. I don't know what my father and mother thought, as they didn't comment. But little Jennifer was impressed. When we did the shoulder lift at the end, she squeaked, "Daddy pick her up!"

I COULDN'T BE A BALLET DANCER, but I could be a ballet dad, and introduce my children to something I never knew as a child.

I took the whole family to Balanchine's *Nutcracker*, year after year. And when Jenny was a teenager I dragged her from New Jersey, over her mother's protests, to the New Dance Group Studio, where she started jazz and modern dance, and after some resistance, ballet. When she was sixteen we reversed roles — I was in the audience at New Dance Group, watching Jenny in the Jazz Workshop.

Jenny was a natural, and I tried to help her every step of the way — paying for her classes, even taking her to her first audition and standing in her way when she saw the other girls and immediately wanted to go home. "They're all better than me!" she wailed. No, they're not, I said, and I was right.

In 1984, when she was twenty, she made a splash at the Jacob's Pillow Dance Festival, break-dancing with a troupe from the streets of New York, under the name "Jenny Jem." She was the only girl and the only white person, two roles that became familiar for her in the dance scene of the Eighties. She went on to dance professionally for ten years, mostly in musical theater.

By this time Mary Jo had remarried and had two more children. On an impulse one year, I took Jenny and her nine-year-old brother Dominick to the *Nutcracker*. Dominick cracked up at the "Tea" divertissement, where the male soloist pops out of a box for a series of spectacular leaps, then pops back in the box. He couldn't stop laughing and talking about "that Chinese guy!"

Jenny followed up, taking him to a few ballet classes. The next year he enrolled in the School of American Ballet, and they chose him for the role of Fritz, the bad little brother in *Nutcracker*. The year after that he was playing the prince! He was the star of the children's cast for a couple of years, and loved being the toast of the town during the Christmas season, signing autographs at the stage door.

Dominick had a short career in ballet — like many kids, he drifted away as a teenager. But for years after that, his picture was on the cover of the SAB catalogue, looking like a little angel at the barre.

NEITHER DEBRA OR I WANTED our little girls to be ballerinas. But I made sure they knew about ballet, and could try it if they wanted. Cassie wanted.

She took her first ballet class at a neighborhood studio, and came home with a forged note in her kindergarten scrawl. She said it was from her teacher. It read, "Cassia goes to ballet *avrey* day."

At ten, when her friend Olga was in the *Nutcracker*, she tried out for SAB, and got in. For the next few years we were

ballet parents — schlepping her to classes, rehearsals, and performances, doing her hair, comforting her if someone else got
the part.

Eventually Zoey followed her to SAB, where she was a star
pupil for a couple of years, before leaving to pursue her circus
arts. But she took her ballet training with her. Zoey performed
for several summers with Circus Smirkus, a youth circus that
toured New England. I remember a spectacular exit after one
of her solos — a flat-out, high-flying *grand jete.* For years after
she left, her picture was on Circus Smirkus's poster — floating
above the crowd, draped between two purple fabrics in an ef-
fortless-looking arabesque.

More than once I was moved to tears at the ballet, watching Cassie frolic as a Polichinelle, or Zoey leaping, leading the
line of Candy Canes. My worst meltdown came at summer
camp in Miami, watching Cassie dance the second violin part
in *Concerto Barocco.* When she stretched her arms out at the
end, I was speechless — crumpled over, flooded with emotion.
Debra comforted me, as some other ballet parents — former
dancers — clucked knowingly behind us. (Debra's emotions
are more in check than mine. One of her classic quotes is, "I
don't get moved by ballet.")

Cassie was in Miami because on a hunch, I drove her to
Newark one year to watch a performance by the touring Miami
City Ballet. We had to drive in the breakdown lane to get
around a traffic jam on the New Jersey Turnpike, but I felt it
was that important to get there. This was Edward Villella's
company, and I remembered him as a fierce, expressive dancer.
Somehow I thought Cassie would like this company, and Villella
would like her. She was small, as he was, but danced big — she
meant every step. He did like her and, at seventeen, she de-

cided to accept an offer to dance in Miami, and leave home. I wept.

— That's the first time I ever saw you cry, said Cassie. She was crying, too.

For five years she danced in the corps of Miami City Ballet, and I made several pilgrimages to Florida to see the company. In New York, parents were considered pests and kept away from the performers. In Miami they were welcome, so I got to watch several ballets from backstage. The energy and intensity when the dancers rushed on, and breathlessly off, was like nothing I'd ever felt, far more electric than any sports contest. This was life, and art, at its peak.

FOR MY FORTIETH BIRTHDAY in 1982, Jenny had given me a pair of ballet slippers. I was too busy to even try them on. But I never threw them out — I'd just stare at them in the closet.

At fifty-five, bored with my job and approaching old age, I finally put them on. It was my last chance. I told CBS I was coming in late, and went to a nine a.m. beginner class at Steps on Broadway. I came out laughing like a man released from prison. I could still do it! My body was rusty but it hadn't forgotten anything — the teacher even complimented me on my knowledge.

I had planned to take one class a week, but this was so much fun I went back two days later. This time, I came down from a leap and felt a pain as if I'd been shot in the calf. I hobbled off the floor. A classmate asked me if I was all right. Oh, yes, I gasped, it's just a cramp. It turned out to be a torn muscle that took six weeks to heal.

As soon as it healed, I went back to ballet class. This was the first of a series of dancing injuries that dogged me for the next ten years. Debra told me I shouldn't be jumping. My response: "Jumping is my life."

My first ballet class at fifty-five was the beginning of the end of my working career. Three years later, when the boss told me my heart wasn't in it any more, he was right. My heart was at Steps and Broadway Dance Center, where I continued to leap, and come down in pain, until I finally gave up in my mid-sixties.

I never regretted going back to ballet. On the contrary, it restored my life. The body-memory of a full *relevé* at the barre — on my toes with arms fully raised, back straight, every muscle and bone engaged in soaring higher — will be my inspiration until I die. It's the very cup of trembling.

19

THE ROAD TO DOTAGE

NSPIRED BY TUTORING AT SAB, I set out to become a teacher of English as a Second Language. I took a certification course at the New School, and prepared to start at the bottom. My first paying gig was as a tutor at LaGuardia Community College in Queens, the borough of immigrants. The directors of the ESL program, two women from Indonesia and El Salvador, looked at my resume and asked what was I doing there. I gave them an honest answer — I thought new immigrants were the most important people in America, they supplied the energy and vision that renewed our culture. They also faced the most difficulties, and I wanted to help. I didn't add that I was a sixty-year-old English major whose skills no one else seemed to need.

I had fun as an ESL teacher, first at LaGuardia and then at Hudson County Community College in Jersey City, where I landed as an adjunct professor with an assist from my son Luke, who worked there in the IT department. Most of my students were not college material, but all of them needed the ability to express themselves in English, and so I set about making up exercises that would bring them out.

Here I drew on the experience of my mother, a high-school English teacher. She loved poetry and had memorized all her favorites, quoting them so often they became part of my inner language as well. She liked plain-spoken poets, like William Blake, Emily Dickinson, Robert Frost. Her favorite poems were short and accessible, like Frost's "Nothing Gold can Stay."

> *Nature's first green is gold,*
> *Her hardest hue to hold.*
> *Her early leaf's a flower,*
> *But only so an hour.*
> *Then leaf subsides to leaf.*
> *So Eden sank to grief,*
> *So dawn goes down to day.*
> *Nothing gold can stay.*

For class, I typed out the poem and then cut it up into individual lines, shuffled the deck and gave it to teams of students to re-assemble. Multiple lessons were hidden in this task, which they attacked with competitive fire. I would patrol the room, giving hints to teams in trouble, and when one solved the puzzle I'd sing out, "We have a winner!" The others would go on, vying for second and third place.

Later we'd talk about the meaning of the poem. What's happening when it says, "Eden sank to grief?" A Dominican girl piped up, "That's where it starts to get interesting!" Then I had them write about experiences of theirs that were best at the beginning. Most women wrote about their boyfriends. But one young Chinese guy began woefully, "This is the story of me and my car." My mother would have laughed at that.

I haven't said much about my mother up to this point, because it's a difficult subject. I spent much of my life trying to separate myself from her, physically and psychologically. My goal was to be myself, not what she wanted me to be. But in the end, I have to concede she had a greater influence than anyone else in my life. And in some ways, she was a great inspiration.

Josephine Caroline Frances Marie Hoornbeek Phillips was the only child of a strict English schoolteacher, Pauline Hassell, and a jolly Dutch businessman, Thomas Hoornbeek, after whom I was named. Jo's parents raised her as if she was the most wonderful little girl in the world, and she repeated that performance with me, her first son, believing in it to her dying day. She didn't know quite what to do with a second son, so by her own account she handed baby Angus to her husband, saying, "This one's yours." That set the stage for a rivalry lasting until both parents were dead and Angus and I were retired, no longer competing for anything.

In some ways it was a good match, my mother and I. It was probably more nature than nurture, because I took instinctively to her teaching. Hers was the aesthetic point of view — she was enraptured by beauty, especially in poetry and music. In London she took me to Westminster Cathedral, where I was wide-eyed with awe. She asked me later what I was so taken with. I burst out, "The organ," and watched her beam with pride and delight.

These and other aesthetic confluences convinced her I was her soul-mate, particularly in contrast to the more down-to-earth characters of Pop and Angus. This made for bitter divisions in the family that became even more complicated when I attained the age of reason, and served notice that I was not her soul-mate in all things. This was poppycock to her. She scoffed at my interest in baseball, telling me when I was grown I wouldn't care for boy's games. Wrong, I said, and I was right. But she thought she knew me better than I knew myself.

Despite our rivalry, Angus and I were natural allies, and we did form a pact for a few years as teenagers, an alliance against Josephine's overbearing ways. She claimed the right to eavesdrop on our conversations and phone calls, and read or inspect anything that wasn't put away. She would comment acidly on anything she disapproved of.

Instinctively, Angus and I would retreat to the bathroom, the only place in the house where privacy was assured, to "sit a spell," to use one of our father's southernisms. (Or "set a spell" to use his pronunciation.) I'd wallow in the tub and Angus would perch on the toilet seat, and we'd sing Everly Brothers harmonies, or make up skits in high-school Latin. We also shot hoops for hours in the driveway.

One night, when Josephine made an especially distasteful dinner — she didn't like to cook, and never learned how — we walked out in protest and spent our own money at a diner. That gave us a feeling of solidarity. Still, though we could hurt her feelings and make her angry, we could never make her apologize for anything, or change.

THE WORST ISSUE BETWEEN my mother and me was sex. She was not at all comfortable with my interest in girls, and found ways to insult the ones I liked. (Her comment on Susan Belink: "Isn't she the one with all the moles on her back?")

I lashed back at her, "You'd like me to be a guppy-eyed cellist." By that I meant she would prefer me as a homosexual, or a eunuch. She laughed, but neither confirmed or denied it. By the age of sixteen I wanted nothing to do with her, fearing that to give in to her image of me would destroy my independence and my manhood. I took off for Grinnell, a thousand miles away, mostly to get away from her critical gaze.

Later, living in New York, I dreaded her visits, and they always set off long periods of depression. I managed to feud with my mother nearly until she died at ninety-four, and she felt bitterly hurt. Meanwhile I spent at least a thousand hours over forty years with two psychiatrists and a psychoanalyst, trying to establish a clear separation between myself and Josephine. It never held.

Now, years after she died, I have to admit I am like her in many ways. I too believe instinctively, "Beauty is truth, truth beauty, — that is all ye know on earth, and all ye need to know." I came to appreciate how she nurtured my interest in the arts, and directed me toward fine writing, music and painting. When I reached the age of reflection in my sixties, I even adopted a little weekly ceremony, bowing to her influence.

Down at the end of a dead-end street in Leonia, near Debra's church, is a steep woodsy hill, one side of a valley with a brook running through it. The stream twists and turns as it runs downhill, forming little pools with flecks of foam, before rushing on to the river below. It's one of the last wild places in this New Jersey suburb, and it reminds me of a wild place in one of my mother's favorite poems. "Inversnaid" is an obscure lyric by Gerard Manley Hopkins, which she memorized and would declaim from the ironing board:

This darksome burn, horseback brown,
His rollrock highroad roaring down,
In coop and in comb

The fleece of his foam
Flutes, and low to the lake falls home.

A windpuff bonnet of fawn froth
Turns and twindles over the broth
Of a pool so pitch-black, fell-frowning,
It rounds and rounds despair to drowning. . . .

Every Sunday when Debra and I arrived at church early, I'd walk to the end of the street to spend a few minutes by the woods and the stream. I'd stare at the water, picking out a "windpuff bonnet of fawn froth" to connect it with the poem. Then I'd recite "Inversnaid" aloud, at first in an affected British style, but as time went on, more in my own voice.

I thought of Gerard Manley Hopkins as an effete poet, imagining him like the "guppy-eyed cellist" my mother would have liked me to be. But I had to admit that while his descriptions were sometimes too ornate, he had a good eye, a good ear, and a poetic passion. I would stare at the black pools beneath the froth, and feel my own despair starting to dissolve. Taking it all in was like a stiff drink of scotch and milk, the good and the bad, my contempt for effeteness along with my love of poetry and nature, my love for my mother along with my resentment. It was hard to swallow but I trained myself to take it as an exercise, a preparation for worship.

THE WHOLE DECADE OF MY SIXTIES was hard to swallow. All my comeback schemes came up short, and though I was eventually able to make some money as a substitute writer at CBS, they had no interest in putting me back on the staff.

When I did work at the *Evening News*, they didn't give me

much to do. One of my few regular assignments was writing obituaries of people that no one else was old enough to appreciate or remember.

When the rhythm-and-blues legend Bo Diddley died, I wrote that while he didn't have many hit songs himself, he "laid down the beat for generations of musicians to come." By then Katie Couric was the anchor of the *Evening News*, and she'd never heard of Bo Diddley. She gave me a fishy look, and said what she usually did when I gave her what I thought was a good line.

— What's this supposed to mean?

I tried to explain, but she didn't get it.

— Is this some kind of musician talk?

— Well, yes. She was dubious.

— Is this gonna make me sound smart?

— Yes, I said. It will!

To be fair, Katie was being ironical — poking fun at her own lack of knowledge about some kinds of music. But she still didn't get it, and read it only because she had no idea what else to say.

She never did get me, or trust me, and the feeling was mutual.

WORKING IRREGULARLY, I WAS ABLE to replace about one-fifth of my income, and a similar fraction of my self-esteem. I never knew how much self-esteem was tied up with my job title, but there it was. Still, I made a promise to myself — when I turned seventy, the game would be over, I could give up the quest for "success." Keeping that promise was hard, like breaking an addiction. You still get the craving at times. But the lust for worldly glory was gradually supplanted by other desires, and I found myself drifting onto another course. It's a woodsy way, where you can float like a windpuff bonnet of fawn froth, down the stream to the lake below. Casting about for what to call it, I came up with a name: *The Road to Dotage.*

EL MUNDO, SEÑOR

I'D BEEN LOOKING FORWARD TO DOTAGE ever since I was in my thirties, living alone on 20th Street in Chelsea, where my landlady was an Irish grandmother, Nancy Kenny. On Saturday mornings I used to take out my fiddle, to decompress from the intense workplace of the week. They had a little back yard behind our brownstone building, and Nancy liked to sit and listen to Celtic and American tunes wafting out the third-floor window.

"Ah," she'd say, "Tom's at the fiddle."

"AH, TOM," SHE SAID TO ME ONE DAY, "I'm in me dotage. But I like it." That was a surprise. I never knew my own grandparents, and always thought of old age as a time of loss — losing your drive, your mental acuity, your memories. But Mrs. Kenny said it could be a pleasure, this letting go of things. And it is.

In the summer of the year I turned seventy, I was browsing in a second-hand bookstore when a title jumped out: *The Delights of Growing Old*. The cover drawing was of a rakish

Parisian, nattily attired and puffing a cigarette. His name was Maurice Goudeket, like me a retired journalist and writer, in his early seventies, with the same lifestyle I was cultivating. With nothing he had to do, he was immersing himself in pure experience.

> *I get up before anyone else in my household, not because sleep has deserted me in my advancing years, but because an intense eagerness to live draws me from my bed. . . .*
>
> *Every morning my coffee has a fresh taste, and this comes as much from me as it does from the pot. There is the paper too, which will put me in touch with the entire world. . . .*
>
> *Eventually I emerge into the street, and of all wonders, the street is the most wonderful. . . .*
>
> *Always there are faces, a sea of faces, with everything they conceal and everything they give away. . . .*

I started a blog, with a review of his book and our common experience. I called it *The Road to Dotage*. In the first entry I wrote, "On a really good morning, it is a continuum of wonder, free from anxiety or regret."

Many books and blogs are written about the delights of growing old. Most are pleasant to read, and easily forgotten, because they avoid the obvious truth — old age may be delightful at times, but it's also the time of sickness, pain and death. Uncertainty grows with every passing season — how much longer you have, what kind of end it will be.

Every year you grow more fragile, less able to deal with stress, more likely to break down. I was hoping for at least five years of active, vigorous life in my seventies. But in the second summer of my dotage, I went down hard and couldn't get up. It turned out to be a herniated spinal disc, requiring major surgery and at least a year of recovery. I'm through that year now, but not all the way back to my active, vigorous lifestyle.

If and when I get back, I'm still hoping for a few years of dancing, fiddling, cooking, traveling, playing with my grandchildren, eating and drinking, and going wherever I want. But an old man has to look beyond this, to the serious business of letting go.

I've let go of work, ambition, success. That was easy. Why was I so worried about success and failure? Zen masters like to say life is *shoshaku jushaku*, one disaster after another, one continuous mistake. Why should mine be different? If it looks different, that's only because I am temporarily enjoying the delights of growing old — happily married, comfortably retired, still connected to the world. But this is a fragile moment, a present built on *mens sana in corpore sano* — a sound mind in a sound body — that could collapse in a second, and surely will decay out of existence in not too many years.

The next phase of letting go is bigger. At some point you have to let go of strength, freedom, life, the world. I love the world and don't want to let it go. I walk out the door every morning, take a big breath and say to myself this is *el mundo, senor*. It's the theater of every one of my adventures; what will I do without it?

WHEN I WAS ABOUT SIX, I asked my mother what happens after we die. She laughed and said not to worry. Whatever it is, it happens to every human being — we'll have plenty of company.

She died with equanimity in 2004, at ninety-four, after refusing treatment for breast cancer. Her last words to me were,

"I'm slipping away to where I want to be."

A few years later one of her grandchildren, a spiritual medium, tried to contact her for advice.

— Go away, was the message from the other shore. Just do what I told you when I was alive.

Obviously, she was occupied with something more interesting than life's little problems.

As for me, I have no idea where I'm going. If it's oblivion, that's all right. Extinction is the same as Nirvana in Buddhism — the highest goal, cessation of suffering.

But I don't think I'm eligible for Nirvana yet. More likely I'm in for another adventure, higher and deeper than anything in this life.

EPILOGUE: APOLOGY

THE GOAL OF THIS WORK has been to entertain — to keep my grandchildren and their children turning the pages, and hopefully earn a place in their histories and memories. Still, one might be forgiven for asking — beyond entertainment, what use is this book? Does it instruct us in any way? Show us a good or better way to live?

The "hero" seems to be a narcissist, and an insecure one — living a vain life, seeking public approval in place of self-approval, never defining himself or his values, letting himself be blown about by the wind. What kind of person did he ever want to be? He gets married and starts a family because he doesn't know what to do after college. His father finds him a job, so he becomes a news writer. He travels around the world, observing one thing and another. He practices three or four religions, and dabbles in the arts. In the end he takes refuge in dotage, a polite word for senility. But he's not even senile, just claiming to be, trying to protect his feckless lifestyle.

In answer to this sort of devastating critique, I must plead guilty to vanity, lack of commitment, and failing to define my-self. I admire people who have serious goals that motivate them for a lifetime. A few appear in the book — Walter Cronkite, Tom Grant, Nelson Mandela, Soen Nakagawa, Debra Given. I admire them because they know who they are.

I was never sure who I was. Early on I came to the conclu-sion that there is no soul, that the human mind is not evidence of an "inner self," but a theater of perception, reflection, and feeling, a constantly developing, indeterminate complex. The continuing existence of this complex, its presence in a single body with inherited traits, a history and a memory, results in a feeling of a "self," even an essence. But in truth this complex is constantly changing, growing and decaying. It's something to hang a name and address on, but nothing permanent or im-mortal.

Because our natures are fundamentally changeable, an au-thentic way of life does not have to be a single-minded devotion to one cause or vocation. It can be a way of adventure, letting yourself be blown about by the wind, exposing the mind to a wide range of experience. In this way you're best prepared to answer the most fundamental question — not "Who am I?" but "What is this?"

That was Soen's lifetime *koan*, which I adopted. At the same time, I never forgot my Hebrew patriarch, my girlfriend's grandfather's earth-shaking refutation: "I believe in the soul."

These I took as twin *koans*. And in the end, I have one an-swer for both.

JUST AS I DID BY THE THAMES as a little boy, in my dotage I like to walk down to Riverside Park in New York and gaze at the Hudson River. Like the Thames, the Hudson is an estuary, an arm of the ocean, where salt water meets fresh water rushing down from the mountains. The Indians called it "the river that runs both ways," in and out with the tide. Sometimes it flows upstream, sometimes down, and sometimes both ways at once, as the tide turns.

All we can see is the surface of the water, but this is enough to light up the theater of the imagination. What is this? It's the play of light on the surface of something we call water, moving, glistening, glinting, hinting at everything that lies underneath. When the wind blows over the water, what moves, the wind or the water? Answer: the mind moves.

What is this? Trees on Dai Bosatsu Mountain, sunlight flashing on the Hudson, dawn dancing in the leaves. But I believe in the soul. And the soul is what lies under the surface, what sets the mind in motion and makes the river run. The soul is not a personal possession, it is the spirit in which we "live and move and have our being," the essence, not of myself, but of everyone and everything, the mind that makes all one.

PHOTO GALLERY

Tom and William, 1944

Tom and Angus, 1945; Angus and Tom, 1972

English schoolboy, 1947

American in London, 1948

Thomas and Pauline Hornbeek, 1930s

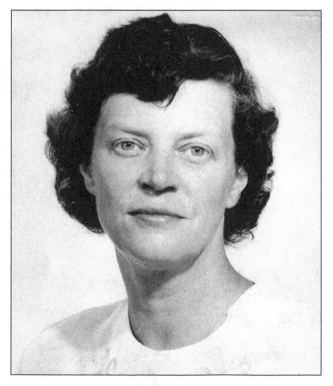

Josephine Hornbeek Phillips, 1955

Grinnell College, 1959

Folk singer, 1960 (photo by Martha Cooper)

Just married, 1979

The Fish Family, 1987—Tom, Debra, Vicky, and Bill (photo by Paul Friedman)

Tiananmen Square, 1989

Charles Kuralt, Dan Rather, and Tom Bettag

Students

With granddaughter Lucie, 2000

Fiddling

Jennifer

Luke

Django

Talitha

Cassia

Zoey

Autumn, 2014